The Land We Call Ohio

88 Counties . . . 88 Paintings . . . 88 Histories

Production Coordination, Editing and Design by John Hoberg, Deborah Bradford Linville and Richard Canfield

History Profiles written by Deborah Bradford Linville

Foreword by Governor Bob Taft and First Lady Hope Taft

Paintings by Richard Canfield, Kaye Michele Darling, Debra Joyce Dawson, Mark Gingerich, Tom Harbrecht, and Richard Otten

Published by Paint Ohio, LLC
in cooperation with The Ohio Historical Society and the Ohio Plein Air Society
Printed and distributed by Baesman Printing Corporation, Hilliard, Ohio

This Book is a publication of
Paint Ohio, LLC
1953 Bluff Ave.
Columbus, OH 43212-3226

http://www.thelandwecallohio.com

Telephone orders 1.800.686.6124
Fax orders   614.487.8099
Orders by e-mail   www.thelandwecallohio.com

The paper used in this publication meets the minimum requirements of American
National Standard for Information Sciences–Permanences of Paper for Printed
Library Materials, ANSI Z39.48-1984.

Printed in Ohio, USA

Publisher's Cataloging-in-Publication Data

The Land We Call Ohio: 88 Counties . . . 88 Paintings . . . 88 Histories/PaintOhio, LLC ;
Project Coordination and Editing; John W. Hoberg, Deborah Bradford Linville, and
Richard M. Canfield; Paintings by Richard M. Canfield . . . [et al] ; county essays written
and edited by Deborah Bradford Linville — 1st ed.

   p.   cm.
   ISBN 0-9746674-0-4 (cloth : alk. paper)

1. Ohio–In art. 2. Landscape painting, American—Ohio. 3. Landscape painting—
21st Century—Ohio. I. Linville, Deborah B., Hoberg, John W., Canfield, Richard M.,
II. Paint Ohio, LLC III. Title.

Dedicated to Lawrence O. Dussault (1931 - 2002)
Marketer, Planner, Strategist, and Friend

Thanking you for your part in what was started,
by dedicating to you, what we have completed.

Thank you friend and God bless you.

Contents

FOREWORD: *Celebrating Ohio*

Dear Ohioans:

As we celebrate Ohio's bicentennial, we pause to reflect on the heritage and vision of the people of this great state. It is also a time to appreciate the beauty and diversity of Ohio's many counties and regions.

It is against this backdrop that six emerging artists have, in the last 18 months, come together to commemorate historic sites around the state, producing 88 outstanding oil paintings of noteworthy scenes of Ohio, one from each county. All of these paintings are reproduced in this book, as is a brief profile of each county's contributions to our state's overall history.

Through the eyes of the people of Ohio, these scenes have been remembered. Through the eyes of these Ohio artists, they have all been commemorated.

There are few scenes painted here that we have not seen, and few sites where the artists have set their easels that we have not visited.

We hope you will enjoy these wonderful scenes, as we have, and that through them, you will take increased pride and pleasure in the fact you are an Ohioan.

– Governor Bob Taft
and First Lady Hope Taft

INTRODUCTION: *The Land We Call Ohio*

The Land We Call Ohio — Eight unlikely people, not knowing one another or the fact that they ought not publish their own book – have come together to publish their own book. Six are artists, one is a former English teacher and one a retired lawyer. We lost a ninth collaborator, a public relations professional, who spurred us on in confidence and excitement until his heart failed and he left us grieving.

Our common desire to record some of the beauty and history of our State during its 200th birthday has been the driving force behind *The Land We Call Ohio*. Ohio is a place where dreams come true – that may be the most constant legacy our state gives to its citizens.

Dreams *do* come true here . . . from the legends of Native Americans – to the carefully compiled historical records of the 18th, 19th and 20th century, Ohio has been a frontier, the "Wild West" – truly the "Heart of it All." For this reason, the citizens of our state have always been encouraged to "Discover Ohio."

Roughly two years ago, Richard Canfield, one of the project's artists, approached fellow-artist Judy Hoberg's husband John, a retired lawyer, and shared an idea for a project to paint the state of Ohio, original oils of Ohio's 88 counties. Richard thought it would be a great project for Ohio artists; John thought it would be a great project for recording Ohio at its bicentennial, *and* a great fundraiser for The Ohio Historical Society. The Society, enthusiastically embraced the idea offering cooperation and assistance at every level, and the rest is, as they say, history.

Richard recruited painters Kaye Michele Darling, Debra Joyce Dawson, Mark Gingerich, Tom Harbrecht, and Richard Otten to join him in painting Ohio's counties. John's near-life-long friend Deborah Linville, former English teacher and history buff, authored historical profiles of each of Ohio's 88 counties. Her historical overviews added to the artists' colorful paintings to create a refreshing historical journey.

The paintings, recommended scenes by local historical organizations, are of historic and scenic interest. A few scenes were chosen by the artists. All were painted en plein air (out-of-doors) in the hot summer, the beautiful fall, the freezing winter, and the verdant spring.

What a varied, beautiful state we enjoy!

Ohio has changed the shape of our nation. Most folks know that flight started in Montgomery County with the Wright Brothers, petroleum thrived in Cuyahoga County with the Rockefellers, rubber became useful in Summit County with the Seiberlings and Firestones. Photocopying was perfected in Franklin County with Battelle Memorial Institute, and space was pioneered by Muskingum County's John Glenn, Jr. and Auglaize

The "Paint Ohio" artists with Executive Director Dr. William K. Laidlaw, Jr. at the Ohio Historical Center, from left Kaye Michele Darling, Mark Gingerich, Richard Canfield Dr. Bill Laidlaw, Debra Joyce Dawson, Richard Otten, and Tom Harbrecht.

County's Neil Armstrong. This book reveals many more things, including where the brown paper bag and the electric automobile-starter were invented; where escaped slaves found friends and freedom; where popular types of apples and corn were developed; where Clark Gable and Cy Young were raised; where huge quantities of water-born commerce were carried in now dry and landlocked counties; where women developed their sense of equality; and where locomotives and tanks were produced that carried our nation's commerce and people and won our wars.

Ohio has spawned awe-inspiring heroes, profound authors, great (and not-so-great) politicians, supreme inventors, mighty businessmen, courageous women, top-billed stars, unbeatable athletes, ethical movements, and reactionary groups. Perhaps Ohio will continue to change the world around us.

Our state is a microcosm of America, its bravest and its best, its victories and defeats, its past and its future.

All of this is . . . The Land We Call Ohio.

PREFACE *and* ACKNOWLEDGMENTS:

In mid 2,000, Dan Woodson, one of Indiana's premiere artists, came to Ohio, along with Robert Eberle and C. W. Mundy to take part in an event that would auction the art of these three prominent Indiana artists and Ohio artists Michael McEwan, Meredith Martin and myself. It was out of this meeting that discussions of the Paint Ohio project began.

Dan shared with me the Indiana story. Five Indiana artists came together to paint all the counties in their state, and to create an exhibit that would showcase them for auction. A subsequent coffee table book was developed. The exhibit was designed around the Indiana Millennium Celebration and the auction benefited the Childrens' Hospital in Indianapolis. It was a great success. He suggested a project like theirs for us in Ohio. And so it began.

First . . . to pull together a team of artists. Indiana had five, we would use six. Indiana had one exhibit, we planned seven–four primary and three regional. Indiana had a book, we would too, and limited-edition prints, 750 each of all 88 counties and a video. All this in less time and with fewer resources. What were we thinking?

The development team began with three people, Richard Canfield, John Hoberg and Larry Dussault (1931 – 2002), a graphic designer, a retired attorney/videograper, and a marketing professional. John was the first to share the vision and added the consideration of a wonderful beneficiary, the Ohio Historical Society. He knew some people there. He also suggested we should do this for the bicentennial. We met with OHS and presented the project. It was enthusiastically approved and strategy sessions with OHS began.

Following recommendations, leads, discussions, interviews, refusals . . . and dozens of rabbit trails, I found six artists. They were all good, and all from central Ohio. Availability for meetings and other considerations required they be at close proximity: Columbus, West Jefferson, Sunbury, and Pataskala. Now we could begin.

The next 18 months included hours of meetings, strategy and planning sessions, PR events, contracts, agreements, negotiations and solicitations. Setting up easels regularly the artists spent weeks and months crisscrossing the state in all sorts of inclement weather. New acquaintances and friends came from hours of communications with strangers. And as a wonderful aside, we came to meet so many great people at OHS from security to the Executive Director, all who were sources of enthusiastic, resourceful help.

By June, 2003, we were ready with 88 dynamic paintings and an exhibit itinerary that included Columbus, Salem, Cleveland and Cincinnati, (full exhibits) and Perrysburg (Toledo), Chillicothe, and Marietta, (hosts of regional displays).

We began a new phase of the project, the back-breaking part of it. Coordination, transport, setup and takedown of each of the seven shows was an unbelievably exhausting challenge. Finally it was done. With its conclusion, we believe we have a wonderful project that commemorates our great state. We hope you'll agree.

I'm happy to say, though, at this writing, all but the auction and marketing and distribution of the book has been completed. The auction at the Apple Tree Auction Center, with the Schnaidt family

and assistants, will, I'm sure, go well. I feel confident thanking them in advance. And, of course, you the reader, who has by your interest in the project and through purchases of either prints or books, shown your support and appreciation for this project and the Ohio Historical Society's fine work in the last 100-plus years. Thank you "Ohioan," you have yet another reason to be proud.

"The Land We Call Ohio" is a project that has required immeasurable effort on the part of dedicated groups of people from a range of varied interests. It is these people who deserve our heartfelt thanks. I salute the following people and their work.

In regard to the artists – Kaye Michele Darling, Debra Joyce Dawson, Mark Gingerich, Tom Harbrecht and Richard Otten – it's certain "The Land We Call Ohio" project has been an amazing adventure, and for your contributions to it with these beautiful paintings that will assuredly offer a lasting legacy to the commemoration of Ohio's bicentennial, we are grateful.

To thank every individual at the Ohio Historical Society by name, as they deserve, I'd need to add pages. In fact, I'm sure there were those who contributed that I never met. I thank them all. In addition special recognition needs to be given to several key people. First and foremost, thank you to then-Executive Director Dr. Gary C. Ness for getting us started. We were fortunate to inherit the support of his successor, Dr. William K. Laidlaw, Jr., upon his arrival in August 2003. Their vision and enthusiasm for this venture has been most gratifying to all concerned. Additionally, thanks to Scott Mueller and the great folks in the Office of Institutional Advancement including Michael Ring, Director of Marketing, and all those who are associated with the marketing machine at OHS, and certainly Bill Mahon in Interpretation/Design and all those in his department who developed such dynamic and practical exhibition and collateral material solutions. I'd also like to say thank you to all the OHS county organizations who so enthusiastically contributed to the successful outcome of the project.

In addition, I believe a special thanks needs to go to the media in Ohio – Toledo, Cleveland, Canton-Akron, Salem, Youngstown, Marion, Madison, Springfield, Dayton, Cincinnati, Chillicothe, Marietta, Zanesville, and of course, Columbus. There are many other secondary markets where the voice of the press has recorded our excitement and passed along the news of our project. It's given people of our state an opportunity to share in the interest of the artists to commemorate Ohio. Of course, this started in Columbus, where with energy and interest, Arts Reporter Bill Mayr considered the project, found it of interest, offered affirming, positive words of encouragement through his coverage and spurred us on. Thanks *Columbus Dispatch* for your coverage. In the inimitable words of my late, good friend Larry Dussault, "Good Work. Good Work!"

– Richard M. Canfield, Project Manager
October, 2003

The Land We Call Ohio

88 Counties . . . 88 Paintings . . . 88 Histories

Adams

2000 Population - 27,330
Land Area - 584 Sq. Mi.
Persons/Sq. Mi. - 46.8

In the unglaciated rolling hills and steep ridges of Adams County, early white settlers found significant evidence of long-vanished Native Americans. The magnificent Serpent Mound sitting on a bluff atop Brush Creek is a 1,335 ft. slithering snake that seems to be devouring an egg. Few clues exist to explain what is considered to be the largest effigy earthwork in the world. Another prehistoric Indian remnant believed to be from the Fort Ancient culture is high on a cliff in Green Township. These petroglyphs are a right and left footprint as well as a symbol of unknown meaning.

Adams was one of Ohio's original counties formed from Virginia Military District lands in 1797, by Northwest Territory Governor Arthur St. Clair. One surveyor and veteran was Nathaniel Massie, who with 25 other families established the county's first white settlement in 1791, Massie's Station. The town later became Manchester, the first county seat. In 1798, the county seat was removed to Adamsville (now Rome), and in 1804, to West Union, where it remains.

The chief early county industry was agriculture; at first the harvesting of timber and tanbark from the dense forest, and later the cultivation of wheat, corn and hay. The main export, tobacco, was especially important.

An iron industry began in 1811 with Brush Creek Furnace; Steam and Marble Furnaces soon followed. By the mid-nineteenth century this industry declined due to depleted local resources and competition from furnaces in the neighboring Hanging Rock Iron region up the Ohio River.

Manchester Button Works used clamshells dredged from the Ohio River, but that industry died because of river pollution and changing fashion.

Zane's Trace became Adams County's first road in 1791 (today's State Route 41). After 1811, steamboat travel became widespread, and river towns like Manchester flourished into the 1870's. With the advent of the Cincinnati & Eastern railroad in 1877, road improvements slackened, keeping Adams rural and remote well into the 20th century. Located off the beaten path, many early buildings and much of the rural beauty of the county remain. Among the treasures is the West Union United Presbyterian Church, the oldest church structure in continuous use in Ohio. Also in West Union is the Old Wayside Inn, formerly known as Bradford's Tavern, where Andrew Jackson met with General Santa Ana to discuss the Mexican War. The Moore's Memorial Chapel in Blue Creek is the original site of the first Methodist church in the Northwest Territory, organized in 1795.

During the Civil War, the 70th Ohio Volunteer Regiment trained at Camp Harmer at West Union. The famous battlefield nurse Annie Turner Wittenmyer was born near Sandy Springs in 1827. Confederate General John Hunt Morgan's forces raided Adams County in the summer of 1863, looting and pillaging as they moved east. They stayed overnight at the Wickerham Inn in Peebles, which stands today.

Adams County is named for our second president John Adams, who was in office at the time of the county's founding.

ADAMS
THE SERPENT MOUND

I guess I felt I had to paint the Serpent Mound. Although some might argue the fact of whether or not it's the most historically significant sight, it certainly is the best known, truly an intriguing sight. Roughly a quarter mile of wandering mound that at any one point is indefinable as a snake. But backing away, wow!, what a feat. Some people call it an effigy — I consider it art. And, since there has been no specific reason found for its construction, who's to say . . . maybe they did too!

– Richard Canfield

The Serpent Mound 18" x 24" Oil on Canvas – Richard Canfield

Allen

2000 Population - 108,473
Land Area - 404 Sq. Mi.
Persons/Sq. Mi. 268.2

It is difficult, at the dawn of the 21st Century, to envision Ohio as the wild and wooly west. Allen County history, nevertheless, reminds us that Ohio was the frontier for much of the 19th Century. Allen County has had it all: battles with nature and battles with Indians, brawling and bad guys, and booms and busts of railroads and oil.

Carved from the Great Black Swamp in 1820, Allen was part of the last Indian lands. When the Native Americans were forced west, a surge of settlers, many from Pennsylvania, arrived to clear the swamps to farm. Fighting muck, stagnant water, and rampant insects to drain the lands by hand, pioneers found the local lime for quinine important in combating fever and disease. Some attribute the county seat (1831) being named Lima for that reason. Swiss Mennonite immigrants arrived in 1832,

in the northeast corner of the county along Riley Creek establishing Bluffton. Their industriousness and tenets of church and education led to the founding of Bluffton College in 1837.

The Miami and Erie Canal was essential to expanding the retail base for corn and wheat crops. Building through the county was a difficult engineering feat for the hand labor. The high point of the Auglaize and St. Mary watersheds had to be breeched. Deep Cut, 6,600 feet long and up to 50 deep, it ended up taking nearly four years of digging by 500 laborers. The site near Spencerville attracted colorful characters and became known for its saloons, liquor, brawling, and the occaisional duel over a woman.

Allen County became a major Ohio rail center in the mid-1800's when the canals declined. Lima Locomotive Works (1879-1951) turned out over 7,500 steam engines, supplying over one-third of the nation's logging locomotives. The factories converted to Sherman tanks turning out over 1,600 in World War II. The Lima Works diversified into cranes, shovels, and road-building equipment when the railroads waned. So many troop trains came through Lima that it also became famous for its servicemen's canteens.

Coincidental with the railroads, the discovery of the Lima oil fields set off a

boom that lasted for decades. After Benjamin Faurot's original well in 1885, within two years seventy wells existed in Lima alone. Allen County was the world's leading producer of crude oil until 1910. Lima remains the pipeline center of the Midwest because of John D. Rockefeller's foresight in building pipeline networks from Lima. Premcor (1886) is now Ohio's oldest oil refinery in continuous operation.

National excitement arose from Lima in 1933, when John Dillinger and his gang shot the Lima sheriff. After a national manhunt for the number one outlaw in the U.S., Dillinger was gunned down in Chicago for this crime.

All good westerns have heroes, too, and Allen County has many. Astronomer Leslie Peltier, Astronaut Robert C. Springer, Physicist/Nobel-Prize winner William Fowler and the Civil War, Angel of Mercy, nurse Annie Turner Wittenmyer are all natives.

Allen County's name origin is unclear. Both Revolutionary War hero Colonel Ethan Allen and Colonel John L. Allen of the War of 1812 vie for the honor.

ALLEN
THE FLATS AT RILEY CREEK

Of all the sights I've painted, this was one of the more comforting for me. I know that's a funny word to use for a painting, but I guess the memory of being there late in the afternoon, early evening, the light was low and almost glowing, the air was still and the only audible record was the occasional bird and the sound of the clear water of Riley Creek as it tumbled over rocks on the high ground of its bed as it meandered south. Thinking about it, it seemed obvious why an early group of settlers (the Swiss-Mennonite people) would have picked this spot to stop.

– Richard Canfield

The Flats at Riley Creek 16" x 20" Oil on Canvas – Richard Canfield

Ashland

2000 Population - 52,523
Land Area - 424 Sq. Mi.
Persons/Sq. Mi. - 123.8

The primeval forest of towering hemlocks and old-growth white pines brings the ancient past into the present in Clear Fork Gorge in Ashland County. The National Natural Landmark in Mohican State Park marks the end of the advance of the last glacier to enter Ohio 12,000 years ago. Glacial melt cut through the sandstone over time, leaving a natural wonder 1,000 feet wide and up to 300 hundred feet deep. Evidence of pre-historic Indians exists nearby from the earthworks and artifacts around the Muddy, Black, and Clearfork branches of the Mohican River. Later, the Delaware, Ottawa, and Wyandot hunted in the region and had towns on the west side of Jerome Fork and at Greentown.

White settlement was slow but steady after the War of 1812. Ashland County was charted in 1846, with Ashland City as its seat. Among the early pioneers in the area, the itinerant John Chapman (Johnny Appleseed) came through to plant and tend apple orchards and lived there several different times. The Studebaker family had a large homestead in the county from 1836 through the 1850's then had to sell the farm to pay their debts. The wagon maker/ blacksmith and his sons had extended bad credit and were known for their generosity to the less fortunate. They moved to Indiana where the sons eventually were among the few wagon-making enterprises to successfully convert to automobile manufacturing. Ashland County also claims the first Ohioan to enlist in the Union Army, Lauren Andrews. He was later president of Kenyon College.

The Brethren Church founded Ashland University as a college in 1878. In the early years conflict between the liberals and conservatives within the church over school issues led to a schism. Finally, the Brethren liberals bought out the conservative branch in 1882 to set the future for Ashland. The University has grown to be a non-sectarian institution with branches and graduate programs in several locations.

Hayesville and Loudonville are also cultural centers with revived lavish entertainment halls to their credit. Hayesville housed the Vermillion Institute, a Baptist-turned-Presbyterian school which flourished under one of Ohio's premier educators, Dr. Diefendorf. When he left, the school floundered, but established its legacy in several alumni. Sheldon Jackson was a revered educator and missionary in the upper Midwest, in Indian Territory and Alaska. Jackson was responsible for rescuing the starving Alaskan natives with revived reindeer herds. He received world attention when in 1897, he sent deer to feed the crews of eight whaling vessels trapped in the Artic ice, thereby alleviating starvation of the crews.

The Hayesville Opera House has been in operation from 1886 to the present. It boasts a long history of stars throughout its tenure. Many of them have autographed the stage walls, including Buffalo Bill in 1888. Loudonville has been restoring its 1910 Ohio Theatre to its former elegance and continues to attract moviegoers and other businesses as the restoration continues.

Ashland was named for the prominent politician Henry Clay's home, "Ashland."

ASHLAND
CLEAR FORK RIVER

We ran two miles along the Clearfork River in the Mohican State Forest until the areas my Dad described of his Huckleberry Finn-childhood reawakened his story telling in me. The yellow river smothered in setting sunlight lit up the trees and water in its radiance and I immediately knew my painting choice. We were near the Little Lyons Falls, which flows into the Clearfork at this point.

– Kaye Michele Darling

Clear Fork River 30" x 20" Oil on Canvas - Kaye Michele Darling

Ashtabula

2000 Population - 102,728
Land Area - 702 Sq. Mi.
Persons/Sq. Mi. - 146.2

First, best, biggest, most–Ashtabula County really does cover many of those distinctions for Ohio. When surveyor Moses Cleaveland and his men located the overgrown Pennsylvania state line marker and struggled on to Lake Erie a few hours later on July 4, 1796, they were the first settlers to arrive in the Connecticut Western Reserve. Although they started their work at Conneaut, Ohio's "Plymouth Rock," the task force initially did not stay because they had to move west for their assignment. Cleaveland's men, however, may have held Ohio's first Independence Day celebration, for they named the spot Port Independence and celebrated with rifle shots, cheers, and much grog.

Ashtabula officially became a county in 1808 with Jefferson as its seat. The county is the largest in Ohio and has its longest lake shoreline. Lake Erie was the economic spur for the area from the early 1800's through the 1970's when iron, coal, and steel came from surrounding counties to be shipped worldwide. Now that the lake is clean again, reviving the recreational aspects of the shore is becoming big business. Geneva-on-the-Lake was Ohio's first summer resort as early as 1869.

Henry Firestone, Henry Ford, and John D. Rockefeller camped in what was considered this remote area in the early 1900's. The town and vacation amenities grew along with access to it; a new state park conference facility is to enhance Geneva State Park.

With sixteen covered bridges, Ashtabula has the most of any Ohio county. The bridge in Harpersfield is also the longest covered bridge in the state. Another bridge, the Ashtabula Bridge, was the cause of Ohio's deadliest railroad disaster when it collapsed in 1876. This tragedy changed the trend of using iron in bridges to using steel.

One of the earliest settlers in the county, Unionville's Colonel Robert Harper, built his estate, Shandy Hall, from 1815-1830. Harper served as a spy making forays into Canada to learn about the French.

Ashtabula ranked as one of the most important anti-slavery counties in the nation. John Brown headquartered in North Andover as he prepared for Harper's Ferry, and much of his ammunition was stored in nearby Cherry Valley. Betsy Mix Cowles from Austenberg strived her entire life for anti-slavery and women's rights causes. An Oberlin educated teacher, Cowles was the president of the first Ohio Women's Rights Convention, the first female dean of women (Grand River Institute), and the first female superintendent of schools in Ohio. As the major northern terminus of the Underground Railway, Ashtabula boasts that there is no record of any slave being returned south from this county.

Many of these runaways in the 1840's stayed at the Hubbard House, which they called "Old Mother Hubbard's Cupboard" before sailing from the harbor to Canada. One important incident occurring here was the rescue of Milton Clarke, the model for "Uncle Tom's Cabin's" George Harris, from slavers, and reuniting him with his brother at the Hubbard's.

In the county seat, Jefferson, ardent abolitionists Joshua A. Giddings and Benjamin F. Wade had their law offices before, during, and after their respective political careers in both Houses of Congress. As President Pro Tem of the U. S. Senate, Wade presided over President Andrew Johnson's impeachment trial in 1868. He narrowly missed being the first such official to become President, as there was no vice president at the time.

Ashtabula takes its name from its river, bearing the local Native American word meaning "Fish River."

ASHTABULA
SHANDY HALL, LATE AFTERNOON

I decided to paint Shandy Hall, Col. Robert Harper's home, because Colonel Harper seemed to have wide influence in the county. Of course as a painting subject, the house's simple shape and stark whiteness in its environment, enable it to hold its own visually, creating some very subtle images.

– Richard Canfield

Shandy Hall, Late Afternoon 23 3/8" x 23 3/8" Oil on Panel - Richard Canfield

Athens

2000 Population - 62,223
Land Area - 507 Sq. Mi.
Persons/Sq. Mi. - 122.8

Education and culture were the raison d'etre for Athens County from its inception. Congress specified land for an institution of higher education in 1802 to be called the American Western University and to be the first college in the Northwest Territory. By 1804, the Ohio General Assembly affirmed the project and Ohio University was born. The name Athens was deliberately chosen for its allusions to scholarship and culture. Athens County was formed the following year, with the city of Athens as county seat. The University graduated its first class in 1815. Surviving years of uncertain frontier hardships, uncertain finances, and student rebellions in various forms, Ohio University has fulfilled the promise of its founders.

Although the growth and economy of the county have centered on the college, other aspects of life in Athens County have followed courses parallel to many other Ohio county histories. The area was home to the prehistoric moundbuilders who left traces of their culture in what became Ames and Alexander townships. Agriculture and mining have sustained the county for much of its two hundred years. The deadliest mine accident in Ohio's history occurred here in Millfield in 1930. At the Sunday Creek Coal Company mine #6, a methane pocket exploded burying eighty-two miners and company officials. Ironically, the company president and several officers were inspecting the safety precautions installed at the time.

The natural resources of coal, shale, and clay spurred economic growth from brick making. Prior to the first commercial brick company in Nelsonville in 1871, brick for Ohio University and other buildings was manufactured on site. By 1900, there were twenty-four brick companies in the Hocking Valley. Nelsonville was known for its salt glazes and decorative features. Streets all over America are paved with Athens County products, including the original Indianapolis 500 race track 'The Brickyard.' General Clay is the sole remaining operation.

Education continued as the county backbone. Coinciding with the opening of the great university, residents made plans to prepare young men for college-level study. Amesville had no library and less money but was dedicated to providing scholarly resources. In 1803, the townspeople sent Sam Brown and Ephraim Cutter to Boston with a pack of animal skins worth $73.50 to trade for books. They returned with fifty-one books for their new Western Library Association, which became popularly known as the Coonskin Library.

Athens County led the way in educating African-Americans with the Enterprise Academy in Albany. Operated from 1864-85, this was the first national education effort established and operated by and for African-Americans. The curriculum was basic, as many of the attendees had little or no previous educational opportunities.

The legacy of fine arts remains alive and well in Athens County. The area became a haven for counterculture in the mid-1900's. Many artists created studios in the hills and have attracted galleries, studies and public projects to the region promoting Appalachian and contemporary arts and crafts.

Athens County was named after Athens, Greece.

ATHENS
NELSONVILLE BRICK KILN PARK
(BICENTENNIAL)

The Nelsonville brick kilns were a beautiful sight to us, after we pinpointed the old boot factory and then feeling unsure about what side road could boast of brick kilns. We found the kilns while traffic sounds reduced to a murmur and we were awed by this unusual sight of brick domes huddled together like old friends on a rainy spring day. The kilns are as welcoming and unusual to behold as any ceramic piece itself could be! What a joy to come upon such interesting little chubby brick characters under the tender trees. An instant painting was found of two old close friends.

– Kaye Michele Darling

Nelsonville Brick Kiln Park (Bicentennial) 18" x 24"   Oil on Canvas - Kaye Michele Darling

Auglaize

2000 Population - 46,611
Land Area - 401 Sq. Mi.
Persons/Sq. Mi. - 116.2

Heavily wooded and swampy, Auglaize was made even more hostile by Native Americans and French and British fighting. The St. Mary's and Auglaize Rivers were heavily traveled fur trading routes from the Ohio River to Lake Erie. The French built Fort AuGlaize (1748-61) near Wapakoneta, which was captured and torn down by the British. General George Rogers Clark drove the Shawnees from their primary town of Piqua up to Hog Creek and Wapakoneta in 1780. By 1782, Clark destroyed Loramie's Post where Jesuit Priest Peter Loramie had come to minister to the Shawnee and Wyandots. Originally a British trading post, Loramie and the resident Indians were considered dangerous so Clark drove them west. General 'Mad' Anthony Wayne rebuilt and used it in 1793. The Post at Girty's town (St.Mary's) met a similar fate in 1784. The Greenville

treaty line runs through Loramie. Fort Barbee outpost (St. Mary's) was a War of 1812 fort, as were rebuilt and restocked St. Mary's and Fort Loramie. They were all used by Generals Harmer, Wayne, and Harrison. Harrison also erected Fort Amanda in 1812 as a supply depot. A granite shaft marks the grave of seventy-five unknown War of 1812 soldiers. Amanda had spurred the growth of a town; the granite monument also marks the site of Auglaize's first shipyard, religious meetinghouse, first post office, and national cemetery. The first white child born to settlers lies in the cemetery. Wapakoneta had an Indian reservation as late as 1832.

Auglaize began to grow with the coming of the Miami-Erie canal in 1838 at New Bremen, which is the mid-point of the canal. Loramie once again showed its importance as the summit of the canal and, therefore, the location of Lock 1 North and Lock 1 South. The contour of the county changed dramatically when Grand Lake St. Mary's and Lake Loramie were dug as feeders to the canal. Auglaize finally became an official county in 1848. The Canal reached its peak in 1852 when four hundred boats were in operation. Today the towpath is one of two scenic byways in the county where it follows Route 66. The forty-seven mile Miami-Erie trail, part of the Buckeye Trail, begins in Loramie and

ends in Delphos. Both Grand Lake St. Mary's and Lake Loramie are recreational state parks.

Auglaize prospered agriculturally with railroads crossing through shortly after the canal. In the 1880's, the county enjoyed the gas and oil boom from the Lima field. Agriculture continues to thrive with its attendant services. Just south of Minster, Dannon Yogurt has one of the world's largest dairy processing plants.

Wapakoneta, Auglaize county's seat, came to the world's attention when native son astronaut Neil Armstrong became the first human to walk on the moon. His stirring words, "That's one small step for man, one giant leap for mankind," are now part of the American heritage. An Ohio Historical Society museum named after him in Wapakoneta tells the space story and Armstrong's particular role in it.

Auglaize is named for the Auglaize River. Its meaning is disputed. In French the word means water clay; in the Shawnee language it meant fallen timbers.

AUGLAIZE
BULKHEAD, GRAND ST. MARY'S

A gusty sky and a high sun brought me to a point across from the Bulkhead of the Erie-Miami Canal where we camped in a state park. A grandfather and grandson sat fishing during my field study work bringing human interest to an important historical waterway.

– Kaye Michele Darling

Bulkhead/Grand St. Mary's 18" x 24" Oil on Panel - Kaye Michele Darling

Belmont

2000 Population - 70,226
Land Area - 537 Sq. Mi.
Persons/Sq. Mi. - 130.7

Belmont County has been a gateway to Ohio and the Midwest for centuries. Before the Revolutionary War the area served Native American tribes such as Miami and Chippawa as a hunting ground. Hostility and warfare met the white settlers attempting to come into the Northwest Territory. After the War, Indians moved farther west and the land opened to newcomers. Absalom Martin and his son started a ferry service in 1794 to bring people and cargo over the Ohio River. Reputed to be Ohio's first settlement, the Martins originally called the settlement Jeffersonville, and then Martinsville, but it reverted to its popular name Martin's Ferry. In 1801, Belmont became the ninth county organized from the Northwest Territory. Among the first who settled here were the Quakers. They are still here with their Olney Friends School and the Stillwater Meeting House.

Zane's Trace, precursor to the National Road, began here and drew thousands of pioneers to Ohio. Most settlers traveling west from the north Atlantic coast states went through Belmont County on the National Road (now US 40/I-70) or along Belmont County on the Ohio River.

Morristown is on the National Registry of Historic Places because its intact main street is a great example of a National Road "Pike Town." Morristown thrived until bypassed by the railroads in the 1850's. The Blaine Bridge, the oldest bridge in Ohio, was built in 1828. It is the largest and last "S" three-arch bridge on the National Road.

Passing through Belmont County for other reasons, "riders" on the Underground Railroad used the Captina African Methodist Episcopal Church, established in 1825, in the center of the African American farming community. One of the well-known "conductors" was Alexander "Sandy" Harper, who now rests in that cemetery. The church continued to serve the area until 1960. Quaker Benjamin Lundy, a noted abolitionist, wrote the influential *Genesis of Emancipation* tract and organized the Union Humane Society in St. Clairsville, the Belmont county seat, in 1850.

Natural land resources made Belmont County prosperous. Coal mining dominated the economy for most of the late 19th and 20th centuries. A marker at Powhaten Point commemorates the deep-mining industry. Running 100 feet below the surface, the Pittsburgh #8 coals seam extends across eastern Ohio into Pennsylvania and West Virginia. The North American Coal Company opened the largest deep mine in Ohio in 1922. It would later become the first completely mechanized mine in the state. Seven shafts operated until the 1980's, when four closed because of the seam's high-sulfur content. The high production needs of World War II created hazards in the mines and there were several disasters. The last deep-mine accident in the twentieth century occurred at Powhaten #1 on July 4, 1944, when a huge fire broke out trapping sixty-six miners. Surface mines became more common than deep mines. The Clean Air Act limits on sulpher dioxide emissions made Ohio coal less desirable, and Belmont County mining is now at a comparatively small scale.

By the 1970's, coal companies began surface mine reclamation by seeding and re-foresting the stripped countryside. Once ninety-five percent forested, these lands now serve as grazing fields for large cattle operations, tree farms and other agricultural purposes. Today's citizens are trying to save Dysart Woods, the last 0.04% of Ohio's virgin forest that remains in Belmont County, from being undermined. Trees twice as old as Ohio still grow in that locale of completely native species. The U.S. Department of the Interior calls Dysart Woods the "most endangered ecosystem in the world."

Belmont County's name comes from the French words meaning "beautiful mountain," which describes the hills surrounding the area.

BELMONT
REQUIEM FOR A GIANT TREE,
DYSART WOODS

Four hundred years ago a seed
chance-fallen grew,
In virgin Forest land that never white
man knew.
In woodland silence it rose and
flourished
By Northern wind was shaped, from
earth and sky was nourished.

Excerpted from "Requiem for the Giant
Trees"

by Eileen McGann

– Debra Joyce Dawson

Requiem for a Giant Tree, Dysart Woods 20" x 30" Oil on Canvas - Debra Joyce Dawson

Brown

2000 Population - 42,285
Land Area - 492 Sq. Mi.
Persons/Sq. Mi. - 86.0

Looking up the hill from the river in Ripley to the Rankin House must have been akin to looking towards heaven for the hundreds of slaves passing through this famous stop on the Underground Railroad. Many Ohio River towns helped in the Abolitionist cause, but Brown County's Ripley was the most famous. The small brick house on top of Liberty Hill was home to the Reverend John Rankin and his family for nearly forty years. Called 'the father of abolitionism,' Rankin founded the Ohio Anti-slavery Society and lived out his principles helping over 2,000 slaves escape to freedom. The Rankins hosted many others helping in the cause, the best known being Harriet Beecher. She met her future husband, Calvin Stowe, at the Rankin's. She incorporated the story of Eliza Harris' crossing the Ohio River from Kentucky on the ice trying to reach Rankin's house into "Uncle Tom's Cabin."

Other Ripley citizens were noted for their involvement in the Underground Railroad. Along Front Street in the 55 acre historic district, slaves first found asylum in Ohio. U.S. Senator Alexander Campbell, Ohio's first abolitionist, lived here, as did Ripley's founder Colonel James Poage. Slaves all over the South knew these addresses in the mid-nineteenth century. Recently the John P. Parker house on Front Street has been designated a National Historical Landmark. Born a slave in 1827, Parker purchased his freedom by paying his owner $10 per week plus interest until he had paid $1,800. He not only helped hundreds of slaves pass through on the railroad, but also led in other Civil War efforts. He recruited troops for the 27th Ohio Volunteer Infantry Regiment, an all black unit, to fight on the Civil War battlefields.

Brown County's most heralded son, Ulysses S. Grant, was born in Point Pleasant in 1822, then moved to Georgetown the following year, where he lived with his family until he left for West Point at sixteen. Grant was the first Ohio-born President.

The earlier settlement of Brown County bespeaks its importance to the indigenous Indians. Not only was the river important as transportation, there was a well-known salt lick in the area. Tecumseh defeated a Kentuckian assault at the Battle of Salt Lick. Indian skirmishes not withstanding, white settlers continued to establish their claims. Brown became a county in 1819 with Georgetown as its seat. Brown County has always been mainly agricultural. Yellow Dent, the most popular field corn variety in the world during the first half of the twentieth century, was developed by county native James L. Reid.

Tobacco has long been a main crop, with Ohio's only tobacco warehouses still being used in Ripley. As farmers have diversified, soybeans have become the leading crop.

Brown County was named after General Jacob Brown, a War of 1812 hero.

BROWN
THE REV. JOHN RANKIN HOUSE AND THE STEPS TO FREEDOM

I looked at 14 locations in Brown County, but nothing really held my interest like the Rankin House. The house sits high up over the town of Ripley. A quiet setting now, but during the days of the Rev. Rankin, it was anything but. In those dark days of slavery, one could, at times, walk across the Ohio River. Slaves were hidden under the eaves near the upper window shown in the painting, and also in the cellar, the entrance of which was concealed under the back porch of the house. I was attracted to the mossy roof, but I felt to tell the whole story, that the painting needed the river, the steps to freedom and the safe house itself.

– Debra Joyce Dawson

The Rev. John Rankin House and The Steps to Freedom 16" x 36" Oil on Canvas - Debra Joyce Dawson

Butler

2000 Population - 332,807
Land Area - 467 Sq. Mi.
Persons/Sq. Mi. - 712.2

Caught between Dayton and Cincinnati, Butler County has often been the way through to somewhere else. Over the ages, many have found a reason to stay.

The prehistoric Hopewell and Adena left over one hundred mounds, more than in any other Ohio county besides Ross. Three Generals marched through on the Western trail to fight Native Americans for the territory. First, General Josiah Harmer tried and failed with an expedition. General St. Clair built Fort Hamilton as a supply base for his unsuccessful foray in 1791. 'Mad' Anthony Wayne used it more successfully on his way to victory at Fallen Timbers. The county seat of Hamilton grew from the remains of the Fort. Population was enough in 1803 for Butler to become a county.

In 1809, the state legislature authorized Ohio's second university,
Miami, to locate in Butler. The town of Oxford grew up around the college. Determined to make it "the Yale of the West," the founders stressed academics from the start. William McGuffey wrote his famous primer while teaching at Miami. Ohio's first female college, Western College for Women, was established in 1853, on an adjoining campus. Today, Western is part of Miami. Both are here to stay.

The Hamilton panorama reminds us of the major industries, American traditions, and many people that have roots there. The Moser Safe Company's products protect much of our heritage. They produced the vaults that hold the National Archives, containing the Declaration of Independence, the Constitution, and the Bill of Rights. They built the Fort Knox vaults. Moser safes even withstood Hiroshima's atomic bomb.

The Lane Library (1866) in Hamilton was the first free public library west of the Appalachians. James A Campbell, Ohio's 38th Governor, introduced the Australian system of voting - by secret ballot. Native son Charles A. Richter invented the Richter Scale for measuring earthquakes. Several noted authors including William Dean Howells (*The Rise of Silas Lapham*), Fannie Hurst (*Backstreet*), and Robert McCloskey (*Make Way for Ducklings*) hail from Hamilton. McClosky was also one of the
painters of the frieze around City Hall when he was a high school senior.

The Miami Canal (1825-1929) fostered both access through the county and an economic impetus to stay. DeWitt Clinton traveled from New York to dig the first spade of the canal in Middleton. Originally to go from Cincinnati to Dayton, it eventually went on to Lake Erie.

Butler County's smaller towns have endured, too, with similar contributions to the American fabric. Chester's pride is the home of the Voice of America. President Franklin Delano Roosevelt ordered the Crosley Broadcasting system to produce and run the world's most powerful short wave radio transmitters. The result was fifty years of American news spread all over the world by what Hitler termed those 'Cincinnati liars.' The facility closed in 1995 and was decommissioned in 1999. James M. Cox, three-term Governor, Congressman and Presidential candidate was from Jacksonburg. It is currently Ohio's smallest incorporated village. Millville claims Kennesaw Mountain Landis, born there in 1866. Judge Landis was the first Major League baseball 'czar.' He was urged by the team owners to restore integrity to the game after the 1919 Black Sox betting scandal. He ruled with an iron fist for twenty-five years.

Butler County takes the name of
Major General Richard Butler, who was killed while under General St. Clair's command.

BUTLER
VIEW OF HAMILTON

What I liked so much about the view of the City of Hamilton was that the entire city skyline was perfectly reflected into the Miami River. It was a lot of fun to make this painting.

– Richard Otten

View of Hamilton 20" x 24"   Oil on Canvas - Richard Otten

Carroll

2000 Population - 28,836
Land Area - 395 Sq. Mi.
Persons/Sq. Mi. - 73.1

Folks are returning to Carroll County to take it easy. Folks who live there are easy to get to know. Life in Carroll County, however, was anything but easy for its early settlers. As one of the gateway counties, this area saw immigrants from Pennsylvania, Maryland, and Virginia crossing the hilly, forested terrain with difficulty. The Native American Great Trail became a pioneer highway for those moving west, especially from Fort Pitt to Lake Erie. Soldiers marched the route in 1778 on their way to Fort Detroit. Travel on the trail was such hard going that instead of waging a planned battle, General McIntosh and his men made several small attacks on Indian villages along Lake Erie. State route 183 roughly parallels the old road from Minerva to Malvern.

Settlement was slow, but Carroll County was formed in 1833 with its civic center at Carrollton (1815). The famous "Fighting McCook" family immigrated to Carrollton in the 1830's. When the Union called for troops, the two brothers, Daniel and John (from Steubenville) embraced hardship and enlisted, as did nine sons of Daniel and six of John. Of the sixteen McCooks, seven became generals fighting in such battles as Vicksburg, Shiloh, and Sherman's March. Five died in battle, including Daniel, but those surviving went on to be leading Ohio citizens, including Congressman and Governor. Their 1837 house in Carrollton is now a museum that tells the story of this remarkable family.

Farming has been the economic backbone of the county, but with little flat land, wresting a living from the hills has always been hard work. Today Christmas trees are the main agricultural export. To get to know the people of Carroll County and its history, drop in any Thursday at the Algonquin Mill complex in Petersburg. This restored gristmill has become the focal point of the community where volunteers meet regularly to share work and stories. Visitors are urged to help with the weaving, building, cooking, crafts, and other activities at any time, but especially during the annual Fall Festival. In addition to the gristmill the grounds have a one-room school, a print shop, a train depot, and the farmhouse. The mill

ground wheat, corn, and buckwheat from 1826-1938. Also open to the public, the Magnolia Mill in Magnolia has made cornmeal continuously since 1834.

Leesville was an important town for the Abolitionists. Frederick Douglas and William Lloyd Garrison were among the prominent speakers at the town hall. The first church in the county was the Quaker Church in Leesville. The town was also a stop on the Underground Railroad. Leesville Lake is a favorite Ohio fishing spot.

Another place to put one at ease is Atwood Lake. This park, as well as Leesville, is part of the Muskingum Watershed Conservancy District organized in 1933 for flood control and conservation. Atwood has become a major recreational area with a full-service resort and conference center. It has two marinas and several public beaches.

Carroll County is named for Charles Carroll of Carrollton, Maryland, who was the last surviving signer of The Declaration of Independence.

CARROLL
ALGONQUIN MILL

It was colder than I have ever dealt with trying to accomplish a plein-air painting. I was standing in a thigh-high snowdrift with the wind whipping by. My hands were so cold they were purple. The paint was almost too stiff to drag across the surface of the canvas. But in the bitter cold, cursing to my self, I thought, "What doesn't kill you only makes you stronger!"

– Richard Otten

Algonquin Mill 20" x 24" Oil on Canvas - Richard Otten

Champaign

2000 Population - 28,890
Land Area - 429 Sq. Mi.
Persons/Sq. Mi. - 90.7

Before county boundaries, before white settlers, before the moundbuilders, before the Shawnee, there were glaciers. Cedar Bog in Champaign County is one of the remnants of the last glacier in Ohio 10,000 years ago. This first state nature preserve is technically a fen, the largest in Ohio. Fens differ from bogs in that they have basically a neutral or alkaline environment, wheras bogs are acidic. With excellent orchids and prairie plants, Cedar Bog has over fifty plant and ten animal species considered rare or endangered in Ohio. Most of the rest of the county is level with rich farming soil. The area near Urbana, the county seat, was an important Indian council site. Colonel William Ward established the town in 1805, the same year as Champaign County. Famous frontiersman Simon Kenton moved here from Springfield and became the county jailer. Governor Jonathan Meigs also designated Urbana his headquarters for the War of 1812. Fifteen thousand soldiers trained here including Kenton; General William Hull amassed his troops here before the march on Detroit.

One of the earliest settlers in the county was Richard Stanhope. He was a veteran of the Revolutionary War and George Washington's personal valet. When he died in 1799, Washington gave Stanhope a land grant of 400 prime acres in Ohio. After serving again in the War of 1812, Stanhope moved to Champaign County and lived a long, prosperous life there. According to his tombstone he was Washington's "faithful chief of servants" and died at the age of 114.

By many accounts the election of 1840 was a memorable campaign. When Ohio's first U.S. President, William Henry Harrison, ran for office, much was made of his roughness and backwoods ways, characteristics that endeared him to people. In Urbana a Whig parade wagon had a painted sign "The People is Oll Korrect." Opponent Martin Van Buren pointed out the poor spelling as an example of Harrison's illiteracy, but the strategy backfired and O.K. became a positive sobriquet in the language. Urbana was nicknamed "The OK City."

John Chapman, better known as "Johnny Appleseed," was an important figure in Champaign for a great deal more than apple trees. He was a follower of Emanuel Swedenborg, an Eighteenth Century scientist and philosopher who founded the Church of New Jerusalem. Swedenborgians had settled in the county and were considering establishing a college. As a frequent visitor to Colonel John Jones, Chapman convinced him to donate land for the venture. Thus Urbana College became reality in 1850.

The famous Ohioans buried in the Oak Dale Cemetery lie among sculpture created by the "Dean of American Sculpture," John Quincy Adams Ward. Ward was born in 1830, and his work in the cemetery includes an Indian Hunter and gravestone of Simon Kenton. His statue of Champaign County soldiers from several wars stands at the courthouse.

Several industries have settled in Champaign County, but farming remains the largest business on that fertile, level plain in west central Ohio.

Champaign County takes the name from the French word meaning "plain."

CHAMPAIGN
CEDAR BOG NATURE PRESERVE

I chose to paint at the southern part of the county at Cedar Bog Nature Preserve. I was particularly taken by the quiet naturalism, the crisp pureness of the water, the variety of flora and fauna and the flickering lights and shadows on the boardwalk meandering through the park.

– Mark Gingerich

Cedar Bog Nature Preserve 24" x 18"   Oil on Canvas - Mark Gingerich

Clark

2000 Population - 144,742
Land Area - 400 Sq. Mi.
Persons/Sq. Mi. - 362.0

As settlers moved west into Ohio, the Indian skirmishes increased on what is now the western border of Ohio. Perhaps the most valiant Native American in this latter settlement period was Tecumseh, a Shawnee Chief who tried to unite his peoples into a final stand against losing their Ohio lands. He was born near Springfield, now the Clark County seat.

A band of approximately 1,000 Kentuckians including Daniel Boone and Simon Kenton came north in 1780 to fight the Indians in the Battle of Peckuwe (Piqua) just west of what is now Springfield. In this largest Revolutionary War battle west of the Alleghenies, Brigadier General George Rogers Clark led the troops to victory over the Shawnee warriors, who included 12-year old Tecumseh. The Kentuckians returned south. The vanquished Shawnees

regrouped and rebuilt their capital, Piqua, north along the Miami River. This battle put a temporary end to fighting the Indians.

John Paul, one of Clark's men, was the first permanent settler, and by 1799 Simon Kenton and six other families arrived to settle in the area. Mrs. Kenton suggested the name Springfield for the abundant springs in the area. Clark County became official in 1818. Population surged as the National Road reached Clark in the 1830's opening access for its goods to be shipped to the eastern states as well as bringing more pioneers through the frontier. Springfield was the western terminus of the pike; the town grew rapidly with inns and taverns for merchants and travelers as well outlets for farm goods and manufactured items. By the 1840's the National Road was succeeded as the main means west by the railroads. Fortunately for Clark County, the train lines also came through Springfield and the area continued to thrive. Ironically, when the age of railroads began to give way to the automobile, the National Road became important once more as U.S. Route 40, which has been paralleled by Interstate 70.

Although the county has remained mostly rural, Springfield became a major manufacturing center specializing in farm equipment from PP Mast and International Harvester among others.

William Needham Whiteley was responsible for Springfield's nickname of "The Champion City" with his invention of a mechanical reaper. In order to convince the Springfield skeptics of its viability, Whiteley let the horses loose and, running, pulled the reaper across the field himself. By the 1880's, his factory grew to be the second largest in the world, next to Germany's Krupp arms company. Whiteley held over 100 other patents as well. Other inventers claimed by Clark County include James Leffel with water power turbines and Roy Plunkett who invented Teflon.

Education has long been important in Clark County. Wittenberg University started classes in 1845. Clark State Community College was Ohio's first technical college. A.B. Graham, school superintendent in Springfield township, created agricultural boys' and girls' clubs for "hands on" rural education in 1902. This effort quickly became the 4-H Clubs of America.

Clark County took the name of Brigadier General George Rogers Clark, famous Indian fighter.

CLARK
GEORGE ROGERS CLARK PARK

I focused on George Rogers Clark Park, The park is crisscrossed with trails and small streams, and a fine lake. I came upon this small stone bridge crossing one of the park's streams on a cool overcast day. I painted on it for two consecutive days of long sessions since the light was consistent.

– Mark Gingerich

George Rogers Clark Park 24" x 30"   Oil on Canvas - Mark Gingerich

Clermont

2000 Population - 177,977
Land Area - 452 Sq. Mi.
Persons/Sq. Mi. - 393.8

People throughout history have thought of the beautiful hills of southern Ohio along the River as a paradise. Clermont County reflects that belief in numerous ways. Native Americans fought long and hard to keep these lands. Clermont was part of the area that Tecumseh and his brother The Prophet tried to unite tribes to recover for their people.

Many of the soldiers who marched through with General "Mad" Anthony Wayne to defeat the Indians were so taken with the land that they returned to settle. One such military returnee was the first settler of record, Thomas Paxton. He had been a surveyor with Wayne and was so impressed with the land he made his 1796 settlement near what is now Loveland. This spot was so ideal that Loveland grew into two neighboring counties and by the late

1800's attracted the well-to-do to its Eden-like surroundings. George Washington favored this part of the Virginia Military Lands and obtained 3,051 acres here. He sent his surveyor, William Lytle, who stayed to establish Lytlestown, later Williamsburg, the county seat. Clermont County was organized in 1800. In 1823, the seat was moved to Batavia.

Clermont was early and strongly connected to abolitionism. Frances McCormick was among families who moved up to Milford from Kentucky eager to follow their religious beliefs in an earthly paradise of freedom and equality. McCormick established the first Methodist fellowship in the Northwest Territory in 1795. At first the families met in homes with lay readers, then were soon joined by the Reverend Philip Gatch, the first Ohio-born circuit-riding preacher. A Methodist Church was built in 1818.

Bethel Baptist Church was also formed specifically as an anti-slavery church in 1798. James Birny, a former slaveholder, began The Philanthropist newspaper in New Richmond, urged on by sympathizers to the cause. He later removed it to Cincinnati so as to be nearer his home.

Thomas Morris was the first U.S. Congressman (1836-39) to speak out and present petitions against slavery. Clermont was the Promised Land for thousands of runaway slaves in the first half of the

19th Century. Over thirty county sites have been identified and marked for the Freedom Trail.

County place names attest to comparisons with Eden: Loveland, Bethel, Felicity, Point Pleasant, Pleasant Plain, Goshen, Olive Branch, Mt. Olive, and Utopia itself. A French group settled Utopia as a commune in 1844, but lasted only several years before returning to France. Next, after being run out of Wisconsin and Michigan, a Spiritualist group settled there. They perished in a flash flood in December 1847, while dancing a celebration by the river. Utopia's biggest days in the spotlight came in 1910 with Halley's Comet. A group of religious thinkers convened in Brussels, Belgium, to debate the signs. They determined that a certain point in Clermont County, Ohio, was, indeed, the center of the Garden of Eden—Utopia. Nothing came of it but what residents before and since have always known— heaven is on earth in Clermont County.

Clermont is named from French for "clear mountain."

CLERMONT STONELICK

We followed the afternoon routing and were delighted to twine through spring forest and be confronted by this complimentary contrasting covered bridge spanning the Stonelick River. The Stonelick covered bridge is set back and surrounded by beautiful homes in forest locations; the bridge created a lovely and utilized historic landmark of times past snuggled in the deep foliage.

– Kaye Michele Darling

Stonelick 36" x 24"   Oil on Canvas - Kaye Michele Darling

Clinton

2000 Population - 40,543
Land Area - 411 Sq. Mi.
Persons/Sq. Mi. - 98.7

Shawnee, Wyandot, and Miami Native Americans hunted and lived briefly in what is now Clinton County, but their main towns were elsewhere. The first white settler, William Smally, had been an Indian captive before he settled here in 1797. Another very early settler was a black slave adopted by the Shawnee. They gave him a valley as his hunting ground; the area bears his name–Caesar Creek. Clinton became an official county in 1810, with Wilmington as county seat.

The largest influx of pioneers were members of the Society of Friends, or "Quakers." An influential group of Clinton women dissented from the larger body of Quakers to join with an Indiana group monthly to support abolitionism which, at the time, the Quaker tenets discouraged. They rejoined the main group in 1850. By the late 1800's, the area had the largest concentration of Quakers in the United States. The first Quaker college in Ohio was founded in 1870. The Wilmington College curriculum has always followed the teachings of nonviolence from John Wolman to Gandhi. Today Wilmington has a well-known Peace Studies Program. They have the largest collection of materials outside of Japan related to the atomic bombings of Hiroshima and Nagasaki. Reflecting the county's continued reliance on farming, the College also offers an agriculture program.

Famed artist Eli Harvey from Ogden was the son of one of the Quaker dissident women. Harvey gained renown as an animal sculptor with such works as the lions at New York City's Central Park Zoo, a large elk for the national Elks Brotherhood, and a brown bear for Brown University.

Port William contributed "Little Gib" as a drummer and courier for Company D, the Ohio Volunteer Infantry during the Civil War. Believed at ten years old to be the youngest Union soldier, Gilbert VanZandt saw action in several battles and Sherman's March to the sea. As a reward for bravery, when he was discharged after three years service, Little Gib chose a pony named Fanny Lee offered by President Andrew Johnson, over an appointment to West Point. VanZandt lived to be ninety-two.

General James W. Denver was born in Wilmington, married a Wilmington girl, and had his permanent address there, but is more widely known for his exploits around the country. He served in the Mexican War, joined the California gold rush, killed a rival in a duel, was Secretary of State and Commissioner for Indian Affairs under President Buchanan, and acting governor of the Kansas Territory. Denver, Colorado, was named in his honor. Many felt he should run for President, but the dual remained a negative factor in the public eye.

The Murphy Theater attracts local moviegoers and large crowds to live entertainment as well as Sunday church services as it did when it opened in 1918. Charles Webb Murphy, owner of the Chicago Cubs during their heyday, 1906-1914, built the theater in the small town to compete with Cincinnati. Wilmington did not grow to rival its southwest neighbor, but the theater has endured good and bad times to be the pride of the city.

Clinton County is named for the United States Vice-president when the county was formed, George Clinton.

CLINTON
BEAUTIFUL DAY

In Clinton County, agriculture plays an important part for the economy: thus I chose a farm. The day was beautiful with a blue sky and golden fields. I knew that this scene would make for a vibrant painting.

– Richard Otten

Beautiful Day 14" x 28"   Oil on Canvas - Richard Otten

Columbiana

2000 Population - 112,075
Land Area - 532 Sq. Mi.
Persons/Sq. Mi. - 210.5

Yellow and black - these two colors have determined much of the growth of Columbiana County. The yellow clay around East Liverpool drew Englishman James Bennett in 1839 to establish a pottery business producing yellow ware. His success drew other English potters and the ceramics industry was born. Half of all ceramics produced in the United States between 1830's and the 1870's were made here. East Liverpool factories were the first to replace the potters' wheels with mechanization. By the 1940's East Liverpool was "The Pottery Capital of the World."

Black hard coal abundant in southeastern Ohio provided the raw material for coke to fuel the iron and steel industry. The Cherry Valley Coke Ovens were the largest facility of the type in Ohio and one of the largest in the United States. The Leetonia Iron and Steel Company built the "beehive" ovens in the 1870's. The company employed almost the entire village from the end of the Civil War until the Depression. Higher quality iron ore from other locations closed the works in the 1930's.

Columbiana's county seat, Lisbon, is the second oldest city in Ohio, sharing its birth with the State, 1803. The town was the organizing point for abolitionist activity in the county, and nearby Salem held the first women's rights convention in Ohio in 1850. Men were in the audience, but only women were allowed to speak. Legend is that John A. Campbell, then a Salem teenager, sneaked in. Later as governor of Wyoming Territory, he caused legislation giving women the vote because he had been so impressed with the women of Salem.

Two historic captures occurred in the county. Columbiana was the northernmost point where the Confederates penetrated due to Morgan's Raiders. In the summer of 1863, after Morgan's band raided across much of southern Ohio, local militia captured them near Lisbon. Union troops arrived for the surrender; Morgan was captured in Beaver Creek about six miles south.

Another notorious outlaw brought to justice in Columbiana County was "Pretty Boy" Floyd. After the Kansas Massacre in 1932, Floyd disappeared, but resurfaced to rob Tiltonsville Bank in Belmont County. Federal agents trailed Floyd to a farm outside of East Liverpool, where he was killed in a raid.

Equally notorious was county-born Clement Vallandingham. He and his Copperhead Party actively opposed the Civil War. Vallandingham was convicted of treason, and President Lincoln exiled him to the Confederacy rather than jail him near his sympathizers. While in exile, the Peace Democrats nominated Vallandingham for Oho Governor. He won the most votes that party ever received, but not enough to win the office.

Lisbon native Marcus A. Hanna influenced national politics as a "party boss" and "kingmaker." He managed McKinley's career and was himself in the Senate by 1897. He died a few months before the Republican National Convention in 1904, where many had expected him to challenge Theodore Roosevelt for the Presidential nomination. Musician Will L. Thompson wrote many hymns such as "Bringing in the Sheaves." Charles Burchfield, one of America's greatest watercolorists, lived in Salem from age twenty-five. Many of his best-known scenes were of views painted from his home, a restored museum of his work.

Columbiana County was named by merging the name Columbus with Queen Anna.

COLUMBIANA
RETIRED - THE CHERRY VALLEY COKE OVENS

I vaguely remember the coke ovens as a boy. They were more intact and had a heavy ominous character about them. But this day, they had an almost serene, garden-like appearance with the light shifting through the trees moving like a visual calliope. The dark nearly opaque waters offered stark contrast to bright blue skies just above the canopy of shade trees.

– Richard Canfield

Retired-Cherry Valley Coke Oven 24" x 20"   Oil on Panel - Richard Canfield

Coshocton

2000 Population - 36,655
Land Area - 564 Sq. Mi.
Persons/Sq. Mi. - 65.0

Mary Harris' name is not well-noted, but her legacy is. Whitewoman Street, the main Roscoe Village thoroughfare, is named for her. The first white woman to live in Ohio, she was captured by Indians in 1704 from her Deerfield, Massachusetts home. Mary Harris married a Mohawk chief in the late 1740's and they settled in what is now Coshocton. Land Scout Christopher Gist named the trail leading into the village for her in 1751.

An unknown woman left a more tragic legacy in Coshocton. Local lore holds that a white woman captive of the Delaware Indians leaped from a precipice into the Walhonding River. She chose death over being an Indian squaw. Walhonding means white woman, and Whitewoman Rock overlooking that river just outside town commemorates this sad event.

The area is rooted in Indian lore.

Archaic Indians hunted and traded here leaving numerous artifacts. Mounds in the county are reminders of the early Adena culture. Later, the Shawnee and Wyandot lived here. The Delaware moved into Ohio as their original lands to the east were increasingly settled. Turtle clan Chief Netawatwees, or Newcomer, settled his village a few miles east of Coshocton where a few whites and Indians were already trading. Newcomerstown became one of the most important Delaware towns until the population consolidated more into Coshocton.

During the French and Indian War Chief Newcomer tried to ally with the English, but the English were slow to aid the Indians, especially in the 1760's when smallpox raged in Ohio country. Consequently, Newcomer sided with Chief Pontiac in his rebellion against the English in 1763. The English overwhelmed the natives and quashed the rebellion. When Moravian missionaries arrived seeking converts to Christianity, Newcomer welcomed them as help for illnesses, and as possible go-betweens with the English.

Coshocton grew to be the capital of the Delaware nation. Chief White Eyes kept the Delaware neutral during the Revolutionary War. His vision was to establish an Indian State that would cover roughly Ohio and some adjoining lands. This idea received early support in the Continental Congress, but White Eyes died in 1778 before it could be seriously considered. Shortly after the Revolutionary War, American troops moved through the area killing anyone thought to have sided with the British. Led by Colonel Brodhead from Fort Pitt, the soldiers killed Indians whether or not they were Christians. The army destroyed Lictenau and Coshocton. Defeated and decimated, the Delaware left the area.

Evidence of France's interest in the area remains at the Old Stone Fort near the entrance to today's park district Built by one of LaSalle's aides, D'Iberville, the French occupied it from approximately 1679-89.

The county grew and prospered as settlers moved west after the Revolutionary War. By the 1820's Ohioans sought faster routes to move goods from the Great Lakes to the Ohio River, the Ohio and Erie Canal Company formed, and the first canal boat docked in August, 1830. Coshocton rapidly became a thriving canal town. The county however, was bypassed as a major railroad center as railroads displaced the canals. Again, major highways were built around Coshocton County, which has never regained its role as a transportation hub.

A movement to re-establish the Ohio and Erie Canal system surfaced in 1911, but the flood of 1913 destroyed that. Restoration of a section of the canal and Roscoe Village have brought throngs of tourists and new life to Coshocton since the 1960's.

Coshocton derives its name from an Indian word meaning "Black Bear Town."

COSHOCTON
WHITE WOMAN ROCK

White woman Rock is a legendary rock where a captive white girl broke Indian warrior and leaped to her death into the river below. This site was on private property and was a real challenge to get to and paint. It was a wonderful experience to capture the evening atmosphere surrounded by nature while contemplating the historical significance of this place.

– Mark Gingerich

White Woman Rock 20" x 24"   Oil on Canvas - Mark Gingerich

Crawford

2000 Population - 46,966
Land Area - 402 Sq. Mi.
Persons/Sq. Mi. - 116.8

From the early settlement wars to the recent wars in the Middle East, Ohio has given many citizens to war. Most counties in Ohio have war memorials celebrating lost lives, but Crawford County has, perhaps, the most unusual. The County memorializes Colonel William Crawford by its name, and a simple obelisk marker in the county seat, Bucyrus, echoes the sentiment. His story demands recounting.

In 1782, George Washington sent Crawford, a personal friend, to destroy the Indians still fighting along the Sandusky River valley. The Native Americans were ready for Crawford's forces and won the Battle of Olentangy, capturing Crawford and a Dr. Knight. In revenge for the earlier murder of the Indian Christian converts at Gnadenhutten, the Delawares tortured and burned Crawford, even though he had nothing to do with the slaughter. Ironically, the officer who *did* lead the massacre, Colonel David Williamson, was in the unit, but was one of the few who escaped capture. A third memorial to Colonel Crawford is along the Sandusky River near what became the Lincoln Highway. Legend has this as the spot where Crawford was captured before being taken to Wyandot County for his terrible end. A lone trail served as a path through the isolated area. The J & M Trading Post, situated some forty yards from the spot, has been a continuous commercial venture since the early 1830's; proprietors have regaled visitors with Crawford stories for over two hundred years.

Crawford County sits astride the Ohio Great Divide. From this watershed the Sandusky and Huron Rivers run north to Lake Erie, and the Olentangy and Scioto Rivers flow south to the Ohio River. The county formed as a separate county in 1820, after the final Indian treaties. While Crawford remains largely agricultural, several industries and towns thrived due to the railroads. Crestline and Galion were both major rail stops from the late 1800's to the 1960's. The Big Four Depot in Galion was the district headquarters for the Cleveland, Chicago, Cincinnati, and St. Louis lines from 1900. Passenger lines peaked during World War I. Freight on the Railroad Express lines continued busy until the 1960's. After a slow decline, the last Amtrak passed through in 1989. As a major stop for so many trains, the towns became known for "whistle stop" political events. Candidates Al Smith, Franklin D. Roosevelt, Dwight D. Eisenhower, and Richard M. Nixon all stopped in Crawford County during their presidential campaigns.

A Bucyrus mural uniquely honors 284 Crawford County veterans with "Liberty Remembers," another war memorial. New Washington has honored veterans since its returning Civil War soldiers formed a band, initially to play for Democratic political rallies. The New Washington Band has played for over 130 years with few exceptions. Reorganization occurred in 1898 and many members took a hiatus during World War I. While not all the players are veterans, their tradition continues to honor the military with many of its selections. The current roster of forty plays outdoors weekly during summer months.

Crawford County is named for Colonel William Crawford.

CRAWFORD
THE J & M TRADING POST ON LINCOLN HIGHWAY

Man, what enthusiasm! Joe and Nancy Everly, the current owners of the trading post that sits along the old Lincoln Highway in Leesville, had a whole lot to say about their county's history and scenic interests. From Colonel Crawford, to the confluence of the Sandusky River, this little cross-roads community is steeped in history and lore that the folks were eager to share. They're proud of their heritage, just ask Joe.

– Richard Canfield

The J&M Trading Post on Lincoln Highway 16" x 20"   Oil on Canvas - Richard Canfield

Cuyahoga

2000 Population - 1,393,978
Land Area - 458 Sq. Mi.
Persons/Sq. Mi. - 3040.4

The one square mile of Cleveland's University Circle symbolizes all Cuyahoga County. Beautiful gardens and manicured lawns reflect taming of the wilderness that Moses Cleaveland encountered when he surveyed the area and created Cleveland in 1796, to be the capital of the Western Reserve. The spelling comes from an error in early maps. The numerous cultural institutions, ranging from art to medicine that have been at the Circle, result from industrialists' efforts to give back to the community they profited from. The neighborhood's diversity reminds us of the county's swing from rural to urban, from wealth to poverty, from calm to chaos and back.

Cleveland grew slowly because its land prices were higher than in the surrounding county. Other towns such as Berea, with its sandstone quarries, drew the settlers. The first African-American arrived in 1809 to settle in Lakewood. Cuyahoga County was chartered in 1810 with Cleveland its county seat, but Cleveland was a stagecoach stop and market town that did not expand until the Ohio-Erie Canal arrived in the 1820's. The Shakers established North Union (now Shaker Heights) in 1822 as a self-sustaining community of about 200; in 1889 the few left merged with the Lebanon group. Brecksville, Bedford, and Independence had gristmills that flourished along the canal in the Cuyahoga Valley. Alexander's Mill was one of the largest using waterpower from 1855-1977. The county's last mill, it is now Wilson's Feed Mill.

In 1870, the first "blow" of Bessemer steel was poured, John D. Rockefeller formed Standard Oil Company, and Cleveland became the 15th largest U.S. city. The iron, steel, and petroleum industries spawned dozens of "smokestack" enterprises drawing thousands of immigrants. By World War I Cleveland was America's 5th largest city. Only the numbers and variety of people who built them matched the number and variety of factories and related businesses. Cleveland is a quilt of ethnicities from the earliest Irish, Slavic, and German immigrants to the more recent Somalis and Latinos. Many city enclaves share a culture such as Chinatown, Little Italy, and Slavic Village. Downtown sports, entertainment, and the arts unite all the diverse factions. Cleveland is land-locked by its suburbs and its "Emerald Necklace" of parks. Designated a national park in 2000, the Cuyahoga Valley is one of America's newest.

University Circle was Doan's Corners in 1796. In 1882, the founder of Western Union donated land and money for a public park and art gallery here. Amasa Stone, railroad magnate, did the same to bring Western Reserve College from Hudson in 1885; Case moved from downtown in 1895. From 1900-1930 Society moguls built mansions along Euclid Avenue in the area.

Cleveland's economic decline in the mid-1900's was evident early in older parts of the city. The Hough Riots in 1966 and the River's burning oil slick in 1969 were low points in city and county history. The University Circle community was among the earliest civic movements to rescue Cleveland with its incorporation as a development area in 1957. There are now approximately forty-five not-for-profit institutions in University Circle; it is a national model for rebuilding. Cleveland's rebirth continues and includes the downtown River Front and the Rock and Roll Hall of Fame.

Cuyahoga County comes from the Mohawk word for "crooked river."

CUYAHOGA
UNIVERSITY CIRCLE, CLEVELAND

University Circle as viewed from the porch of the Cleveland Museum of Art provided an inspiring spot for me to paint this county. The warm spring sunshine beamed down in front and overhead, causing a halo effect on the various elements.

– Mark Gingerich

University Circle, Cleveland 24" x 36"   Oil on Canvas - Mark Gingerich

Darke

2000 Population - 53,309
Land Area - 600 Sq. Mi.
Persons/Sq. Mi. - 88.9

United States efforts to pacify the Ohio frontier were long and brutal. When Chief Little Turtle defeated General St. Clair in 1791 in today's Mercer County, Fort Jefferson in Darke County became a refuge for the survivors. President Washington then sent General "Mad" Anthony Wayne to the territory. In 1793, Wayne ordered the largest fortification on the western frontier to be built, Fort Green Ville. When Wayne's troops subdued the Native Americans by 1795, twelve tribes came to sign the Greenville Treaty ceding their lands to the U.S. and clearing the way for settlement. The fort burned down in 1796, and pioneers used the nails to build the town of Greenville. Peace was not yet assured, however. When the War of 1812 broke out, troops rebuilt and garrisoned the stockade. Greenville Treaty holdout, Tecumseh, was finally

defeated, and the second treaty of Greenville was signed in 1813. Greenville became the county seat when Darke County was organized in 1817.

Agriculture has been the cornerstone of the county's economy. Extremely fertile till soil, left by the glaciers, and drained swampland makes Darke first in Ohio production of corn and soybeans and second in hogs. Business enterprises support farming. Bear's Mill (1845), for example, is one of the only mills with a turbine engine still working. Railroads came to the region in the 1850's to open markets for agricultural products. The rail center is Union City, which straddles the Indiana state line. Union City is really two different towns, each with its own government and school system, on either side of State Line Road.

Darke County boasts several famous citizens. Phoebe Ann Mosey, born near Willowdell in 1860, took the stage name "Annie Oakley" when she began her show business career. When fifteen years of age, she beat Frank Butler in a Cincinnati shooting contest and married him a year later. Together they toured the world in Buffalo Bill Cody's Wild West Show. She met Queen Victoria and Kaiser Wilhelm. Sitting Bull honored Annie's skill by adopting her and naming her "Mochin Wytony's Cecilia," Little Sure Shot. She and Butler died within weeks of each other and are buried in

Darke County's Brock Cemetery.

Lowell Thomas, born in Woodington in 1892, was a renowned news correspondent during World Wars I and II and later. The world adventurer had a national radio program from 1930-76. Generations knew him as the voice of Fox Movietone news. Thomas made many films and endorsed Cinerama and television, but preferred radio because he could go on location to broadcast.

Another adventurer born in Darke County, Zachary Lansdowne, pioneered the use of helium in dirigibles. He piloted the Navy airship Shenandoah, the first airship to use helium instead of hydrogen. After several safe voyages, the Shenandoah was caught in a heavy storm and the control cabin broke off, killing Lansdowne and six others.

Darke County is named for Revolutionary War hero General William Darke.

DARKE
BEAR'S MILL

Homeland of Tecumseh and Annie Oakley, Bear's Mill was the only location that was recommended to me by Darke County. Built in 1849, this is one of the only turbine mills in Ohio that is still a working mill. I was disappointed by the brand new hickory siding - the original siding was 150 years old. The new siding didn't speak to me of age. Inside, on the third floor, you can see the huge millstones which were purchased in France and brought to this country by ship - a two-month process. I made four trips to this county, three to paint. This painting is the last of three I painted. For me, Bear's Mill was a "bear" to paint. Still, it's a great piece of history, and I'm glad that the community and the owners have worked to keep it in shape, preserving it for future generations.

– Debra Joyce Dawson

Bear's Mill 18" x 24" Oil on Canvas - Debra Joyce Dawson

Defiance

2000 Population - 39,500
Land Area - 411 Sq. Mi.
Persons/Sq. Mi. - 96.1

Service is important to Defiance County. From serving Colonial troops to the service of learning, this county and its people have served Ohio and the nation. One of the counties in northwest Ohio formed from the Great Black Swamp lands, Defiance was created from Williams County in 1845, when the local citizens defied the change of the county seat from Defiance to Bryan. Forming the new county returned commercial and legal clout to the county center at the confluence of the Maumee and Auglaize Rivers where it had been since prehistory.

Native American commerce and settlements had followed the four rivers of the area: Maumee, Auglaize, Tiffin, and St. Joseph. The great Chief Pontiac was born near the town of Defiance. When the French surrendered their claims to the area to the British in 1763,

Pontiac defied the orders and kept on fighting for their land. Shawnee, Wyandot, Ottawa, Miami, and other tribes had used the region for travel and hunting. Generals Harmer and St. Clair attempted to claim the land for the new United States, but were soundly defeated by Little Turtle and Blue Jacket in 1790-91.

Weary but determined to prevail in the West, George Washington sent General "Mad" Anthony Wayne against the Indians. Wayne built Fort Defiance at the confluence of the Auglaize and Maumee Rivers in 1794. One of his officers observed that this fort was strong enough to defy the English, the Indians, and "all the devils in hell." Fort Defiance was a rough square with roundhouses and an eight-foot deep moat with earthen walls fifteen feet thick. From this barricade Wayne's troops did, in fact, win the Battle of Fallen Timbers which was the decisive battle leading to the Treaty of Greenville. Although the Fort was within the lands ceded to the Indians by the treaty, they allowed the white settlers to continue using it as a trading post and fort. Fort Defiance also served General William Henry Harrison in his attacks against the British and Indians in the War of 1812.

The rivers, which first served the settlers, were joined by two canals, the Wabash - Erie, and the Miami - Erie finished in 1847. These waterways

simplified transporting farm goods to distant markets and Defiance became a boomtown. Railroads supplanted the canals as the main commercial transportation that continued to support the rural economy. Now highways and motor vehicles dominate. The county's largest employer is General Motors, which operates one of the world's largest metal casting plant there, and new highway construction through the county will enable Defiance to continue service as a major transportation hub.

Crowning the service orientation of Defiance County is Defiance College. Founded in 1850 as a female seminary, it expanded into a liberal arts college in 1903. Known nationally for its service-learning component, the college integrates volunteering in the community into each of its majors. The program has become a national education model with its volunteer center and five neighborhood centers for tutoring children all run by Defiance College students.

Defiance County is named for Fort Defiance.

DEFIANCE
FORT DEFIANCE

Fort Defiance sits on the confluence of the Maumee and Auglaize Rivers. I chose a view across the Maumee. I noticed how green the grass was contrasted with the leafless trees of early spring. Fort Defiance is a very nice park with an interesting viewpoint.

– *Tom Harbrecht*

Fort Defiance 24" x 36"   Oil on Canvas - Tom Harbrecht

Delaware

2000 Population - 109,989
Land Area - 442 Sq. Mi.
Persons/Sq. Mi. - 248.6

As one of the central Ohio counties, Delaware County has always been a crossroads and gathering place. That legacy as meeting place of disparate people and events continues because Delaware is Ohio's and one of the nation? fastest-growing county.

Olentangy Caverns was a meeting place for Native Americans between and among the Wyandot and Delaware who shared the area. Wyandot Chief Leatherlips made his winter headquarters at the caverns; many say his spirit still haunts the cavern's tiers. Leatherlips' story is a sad one. He was among the Indians who refused to fight against the white man and was especially helpful to the early white settlers who began arriving in 1801. When the Shawnee Chief Tecumseh and his brother The Prophet tried to unite the tribes to reclaim their homelands, Leatherlips would not join. In return, dissident Wyandots condemned him for witchcraft. In 1810, they captured and tried him; the settlers with him tried in vain to help, but he accepted his fate with dignity. Many assert that Leatherlips was executed for his friendship with the whites, not true witchcraft.

One of the features of Delaware that attracted Native Americans and white settlers alike were the mineral springs. In 1833, to capitalize on the spa fashion, Columbus Kent and Thomas Hall developed the Delaware sulfur springs into a resort with the Mansion House Hotel as its centerpiece. The scene was depicted in the 1830's Staffordshire china spa pattern. The bucolic experiment was short-lived, however. A recession forced closure in 1837.

The Methodist Church chose Delaware as the site of Ohio Wesleyan University in 1842. It was originally housed in Mansion House, renamed Elliott Hall. Fully restored today, Elliott is Ohio's oldest collegiate Greek revival building. A premier liberal arts institution, Ohio Wesleyan claims several renowned alumni. Branch Rickey integrated professional baseball in 1947 when he signed Jackie Robinson to play for the Brooklyn Dodgers and become the first African American to play in the Major Leagues. Mildred Gillis, alias "Axis Sally," was an infamous radio personality who spewed German propaganda to the American troops during World War II. Lucy Webb Hayes was one of OWU's first female students. As the wife of Delaware native son Civil War General and President Rutherford B. Hayes (1822-93), "Lemonade Lucy," nicknamed for her temperance stance, was the first college-educated First Lady. Hayes himself had been raised at his parents distillery on part of what is now OWU's main campus.

Northern Westerville was a key stop on the Underground Railway. Runaway slaves were passed among several Sharp family homes along Africa Road assisted by Bishop William Hanby and Lewis Davis before moving north and into Canada.

During the Civil War, Camp Delaware mustered soldiers for the Union army. The Camp divided in two with the west side of the Olentangy river being for white recruits and the east for blacks. In 1863, the first Ohio Black regiment formed here, the 127th Regiment of Ohio Volunteer Infantry.

"Big Ear," Ohio's largest radio telescope, was near Perkins Observatory south of Delaware City, 1986-98. The 340' x 70' scientific instrument listened for extra-terrestrial radio transmissions. Over 20,000 discrete radio sources were collected including the "WOW" message, so-called from its finder's notation, which is unique in radio astronomy. The station was dismantled in 1998, but a plaque honors the project location.

In 2003 Ostrander native Ben Curtis, ranked 396 on the PGA tour, stunned the world by winning the British Open. He learned the game at Mill Creek Golf Club, built by his grandfather and operated by his parents.

Delaware was named for the Delaware Indians.

DELAWARE
ELLIOTT HALL,
OHIO WESLEYAN UNIVERSITY

With this painting, my attention focused on the westwardly setting sun. I wanted to describe what Elliott Hall felt like in the late August afternoon.

– Richard Otten

Elliott Hall, Ohio Wesleyan University 20" x 28" Oil on Canvas - Richard Otten

Erie

2000 Population - 79,551
Land Area - 255 Sq. Mi.
Persons/Sq. Mi. - 312.1

The Erie, or "cat nation," was an offshoot of the Iroquois that did not join the Five Nations. Conquered by their larger related tribe by 1665, the Erie vanished from the area. Subsequently, the Iroquois, Seneca and Wyandot occupied Erie County shore lands and islands until settlers moved in after the War of 1812. Formed from the Firelands of the Connecticut Reserve, Erie County was chartered in 1838 with Sandusky as its county seat.

Situated at the mouths of rivers flowing into Lake Erie, Huron and Sandusky grew into bustling port towns during the 1820-30's. Huron was the leading builder of steamships on the lake. Bypassed by the canal system, Huron did not revive until the railroads took over major shipping in the late 1800's. Milan was the county canal town and was an important grain port. The town has more fame as the birthplace of Thomas A. Edison. He lived there until he was seven years old when the family moved to Michigan. Their house is now a museum.

Sandusky, which means "at the cold water," thrived as the major fresh-water fish market with over fifty commercial fishermen at one time. Auxiliary industries such as fertilizer and ice harvesting were also dependent on the water. In 1826, the first Ohio chartered railroad was begun in Sandusky by lawyer and politician Eleutheros Cooke. The Mad River and Lake Erie Railroad followed much the same route as the Miami and Erie Canal, and along with other rail systems contributed to the demise of the canals. Cooke, who became a Congressman, was the father of notorious financier Jay Cooke. Sandusky city leaders wanted their town to reflect their wealth and culture, so they laid out the city in the compass-and-carpenter's square design of the Masons, a secret society important among U.S. Colonial leaders. Sandusky claims the largest collection of limestone buildings in Ohio.

Several Lake Erie islands are part of the county. Johnson's Island was a Union prison during the Civil War. It housed approximately 3,000 Confederate Soldiers for four years, and the small cemetery holds a number who died there.

Kelley's Island had at least two Indian villages. Inscription Rock, a petrograph that apparently details tribal life, is an Erie legacy. The Kelley brothers bought most of the island from the Connecticut Reserve. The island economy has varied with limestone quarrying, hogs, winemaking, logging, and fruit growing. The wine industry faltered during prohibition, but has made a comeback. Kelley's Island is now a favored vacation spot. The 375 permanent residents host thousands of visitors each summer. There are numerous parks, biking and hiking trails, camping and, of course, fishing at the "walleye capital of the world." Glacial Grooves park was formed when the mile-high Wisconsin Glacier gouged this geologic wonder more than 30,000 years ago.

By the late 1800's people had more leisure time and disposable income. Cedar Point jutting into Sandusky Bay developed into a recreation Mecca. What began as a beer garden and bathhouse in 1870 has grown into a huge amusement super park. Weathering the ups and downs of changing tastes from dance pavilions to thrill rides and lake pollution, Cedar Point now claims to have the most rides and roller coasters on the planet and draws over three million people annually.

Erie County takes its name from the Erie tribe.

ERIE
SUNSET CEDARS ON KELLEY'S

Beautiful Kelley's Island, is a wonderland of paintings and tales of the mariner's life. The color of the sun setting on large cedars along with a misty island atmosphere made my painting a quick field study, and later into a larger painting. I loved the spontaneous scenes of this enchanting place and had to force myself to stop painting sites, ultimately.

– Kaye Michele Darling

Sunset Cedars on Kelley's 24" x 30"   Oil on Panel - Kaye Michele Darling

Fairfield

2000 Population - 122,759
Land Area - 505 Sq. Mi.
Persons/Sq. Mi. - 243.0

At the edge of ancient glaciers, the rolling hills of Fairfield retain many happy accidents of geological change. Eight nature preserves show us today about evolving land, water, plants and animals. Buckeye Lake contains an Ice Age floating cranberry bog, Wakeena Nature Preserve shows rock strata and primeval hemlocks, and the others display eons of biological diversity. Prehistoric Native Americans left traces of their culture with earthworks; Tarleton Mound is the only known mound in the shape of a cross.

Ebenezer Zane opened the county to settlement by routing his road through the area. Fairfield became a county in 1800 – before statehood; Lancaster, the county seat. As the "Gateway to the Hocking Hills," Fairfield was ideally situated for farming and manufacturing. Wealth came and went quickly for risk-takers. Lancaster became a center for businesses dealing in resources and manufactured products such as glass from the Anchor Hocking and the Lancaster Colony companies. Many beautiful homes survive from the 1820's-30's land speculation. The Panic of 1838 caused huge business losses; many speculators left or went bankrupt, but their architectural legacy survives.

The county thrived from major transportation routes for goods and services. Buckeye Lake, formerly the Great Buffalo Swamp, was excavated for the Ohio-Erie Canal and renamed Licking Reservoir in 1827. The Deep Cut through the Licking Summit ends at Millersport, 317' above Lake Erie, 413' above the Ohio River. The Lancaster lateral canal linked the town to the larger waterway. The railroads arrived in the mid-1800's. From 1904-29 the Scioto Valley Traction Company had an interurban line to Columbus.

Fairfield nurtured a number of important Americans. Rushville's Benjamin Hanby wrote the popular Civil War-era song "Darling Nelly Gray," inspired by a story from one of the runaway slaves his abolitionist father helped through the Underground Railway. Thomas Ewing, Jr., a Lancaster native, became an eminent lawyer in Kansas, Washington, D.C., and New York. He saved Dr. Mudd, John Wilkes Booth's unknowing doctor, from being hanged. Richard Felton Outcault of Lancaster was a cartoonist who worked for both Hearst and Pulitzer newspapers in New York. In 1896 he developed the first tinted cartoon, the "Yellow Kid," to test a yellow ink for the paper. Its ensuing popularity spawned a newspaper feud and the pejorative term, "Yellow Journalism."

The Sherman brothers from Lancaster changed the world. General William Tecumseh Sherman sent Union troops marching through Georgia, destroying a 60-mile wide swath to Savannah to South Carolina. Sherman is credited with starting "Total War" and reportedly asserted that "War is hell." After commanding the U.S. Army from 1873-87, he rejected a Republican draft for President, saying, "If nominated, I will not run; if elected, I will not serve." Younger brother U.S. Senator John was chief sponsor of the Sherman Antitrust Act of 1890, the first major effort to control the burgeoning power of monopolistic trusts like Cleveland's Standard Oil Company. The Sherman Act legislated against "conspiracy," "restraint of trade" and "attempt to monopolize," and put the U.S. on a path of regulating capitalism, rather than rejecting capitalism as Europe often did through Socialism and Communism.

General Arthur St. Clair named Fairfield County for the beauty of its "fair fields."

FAIRFIELD
EAST MAIN STREET

Just outside of Lancaster on State Route 22, I came across a glorious vision for a painting. A field of golden color met another of beautiful green at a moment where two trees kept the fields divided. It was this beautiful scene which I was compelled to paint.

– Richard Otten

East Main Street 14" x 28"   Oil on Canvas - Richard Otten

Fayette

2000 Population - 28,433
Land Area - 407 Sq. Mi.
Persons/Sq. Mi. - 69.9

Glaciers moved over much of Ohio leaving flat, fertile land when the last one receded approximately 10,000 years ago. Fayette County is blessed with till, the mixture of sand, silt and gravel, which filled in and leveled most of the valleys as the ice retreated. The glacier also created Paint Creek, the longest creek in Ohio.

Originally part of the Virginia Military District, Fayette County was founded in 1810. When the Virginia Revolutionary War veterans claimed their Ohio land, they hired surveyors often allotting a portion of the land as payment. Jesse Milliken, one of the surveyors, settled in Washington, the county seat. He was the town's first postmaster and clerk of the common pleas court. In the Virginia fashion, when the first session of court was held here in 1810, Milliken added Court House to the town's name. A later courthouse building became notorious from the Riot of 1894. William "Jasper" Dolby, an African-American, was charged with raping a local white woman. When he was taken to the courthouse for trial, a lynch mob gathered. Alarmed officials asked Governor McKinley to send national guardsmen. Dolby was convicted, but the next day before he could be removed to jail, the crowd attacked the courthouse trying to batter in the doors. After several warnings, the guardsmen inside fired through the doors into the crowd. The incident ended with six men dead and ten wounded. Dolby was safely taken to Columbus to serve his sentence. The holes in the "Swiss Cheese" doors are still visible today.

The county courthouse is noted for artistic reasons as well. Ohio-born painter of the famous "Spirit of "76," Archibald M. Willard, painted three murals on the walls. They all feature stylized female "spirits :" "The Spirit of the US Mail," "The Spirit of Electricity," and "The Spirit of the Telegraph."

Farming has defined the county and it remains ninety-five percent agricultural today. Sheep and the small woolen industries of the early nineteenth century gave way to hogs. Fayette County, however, really became most noted for horse breeding, training, and racing. As the Ohio leader of standardbreds, some of the top horses in the nation come from Fayette farms. The largest horse sales barn in the world was built in Washington Court House where buyers came from around the world. Some of the harness racing legends grew up here. Adios Butler was the first Triple Crown winning pacer. The Czar of Russia bought Glenwood M that became the first county horse shipped abroad. The driver of Sleepy Tom, a blind trotter, designed the mobile starting gate. The story goes that "Uncle" Steve Phillips bought the horse for $7.50 and a bottle of whiskey. That investment was minuscule for Phillips who earned as much as $15,000 in purse money for one day at a Chicago racetrack in 1870.

Markers in the fairground infield commemorate champion sire Bobby Burns and his offspring Major Mallow buried there in 1913. Midland Acres in Bloomburg remains one of the largest standardbred farms in the country still holding sales to an international crowd.

Fayette County was named for the Revolutionary War Hero Marquis de LaFayette.

FAYETTE
PAINT CREEK AT DUSK

Early evening sun painted huge fields of color toward the outlet of the rambling Paint Creek which was a deep blue respite of the summer's overgrowth around this baby creek that called for several quiet field paintings from several directions.

– Kaye Michele Darling

Paint Creek at Dusk 18" x 24"   Oil on Canvas - Kaye Michele Darling

Franklin

2000 Population - 1,068,978
Land Area - 540 Sq. Mi.
Persons/Sq. Mi. - 1,980.1

Columbus, Ohio's capital and Franklin County's seat, is the heart of the heartland. Franklin has seen much of the growth and change that shaped Ohio, from Indian Wars to campus riots, but avoided substantial heavy industry. The business of Columbus has been education and government; most fighting in the county has been political.

Prehistoric Adenas left many mounds, mostly gone. By 1763, Woodland Indians lived at the confluence of the Olentangy and Scioto Rivers in Salt Lick Town. White traders tried to establish a trading post there, but were killed within months by Pontiac's uprising. In 1774, American Colonel Crawford destroyed three Wyandot villages on the rivers, followed by more skirmishes from 1775 - 80. Peace then prevailed.

Surveyor Lucas Sullivant platted Franklinton and opened a land office in 1797 on the Scioto's west bank. It became county seat in 1803, the year James Kilbourne named his new town after Thomas Worthington, hoping to lure the state capital there. Siting the permanent state capital was hotly contested by several towns. When four Franklinton men offered land and money to build a capitol and penitentiary on the Scioto's east banks, the Legislature named Columbus the capital. It was the first city built specifically to be a state capital. The first brick statehouse burned in 1852, but was already being replaced by today's Doric-inspired limestone capitol. Architectural competition, bickering legislators, convict labor, and malaria extended construction from 1839 to 1861. In 1865, President Lincoln's body lay in State in the rotunda, with 10,000 mourners lined around the Statehouse block.

Transportation advances from the National Road, canals, railroads, airlines and Interstate highways fueled Franklin County. Columbus was the eastern airport for the first transcontinental train-plane-train-plane "flight" in 1929. Agriculture, always Ohio's top industry, has long been served by the State Fair, boasting many of the nation's largest livestock shows. The Ohio Agricultural and Mechanical Institute, formed in 1873 was renamed The Ohio State University in 1878 to enable the inclusion of a liberal arts curriculum. OSU claims many great athletes, including Jesse Owens, first American to win four Olympic Gold Medals (1936), and county natives Jack Nicklaus, legend of golf, and football great Archie Griffin, only two-time Heisman Trophy winner. OSU's main campus is the largest in the nation; 11 institutions of higher education are in Franklin County. Academic-related industries such as Battelle Memorial Institute, developer of photocopying, and Chemical Abstracts are world renowned for research and development.

Franklin County's war record exemplifies Ohio's national role. World War I top-ace Eddie Rickenbacker and World War II and Cold War bomber commander Curtis LeMay both were born in Columbus. Camp Chase on Columbus' west side was the Union's largest POW camp, imprisoning 8,000 Confederates in 1863 and leaving 2,200 in the site's cemetery. Fort Hayes was a major army installation from 1861 until the 1960's; it now houses an arts and academic high school and career center. Bexley's Camp Bushnell trained soldiers for the Spanish American War; Camp Willis in Upper Arlington to fight Poncho Villa. Columbus Depot (1918) became the world's largest military supply center during World War II, and now serves all branches as Defense Supply Center Columbus.

Franklin County was named for Founding Father Benjamin Franklin.

FRANKLIN
COLUMBUS
FROM CONFLUENCE PARK

On first seeing this view of the city at this time of day from Confluence Park, I was awestruck. This was many years ago and I am glad that I finally got to put it down on canvas. The last glimpses of the setting sun to my back were being gently reflected by the buildings as the lights inside were being beckoned out against the ever-darkening sky.

–Mark Gingerich

Columbus from Confluence Park 18" x 24"   Oil on Canvas - Mark Gingerich

Fulton

2000 Population - 42,084
Land Area - 407 Sq. Mi.
Persons/Sq. Mi. - 103.5

"Everything old is new again" in Fulton County. Farmland for most of its settled years, in Fulton industry and suburbia now encroach on the rural landscape. The steel industry that first built in the oldest Ohio River counties and northeast Ohio and then left those areas decades ago, is the new economic impetus in Fulton and northwest Ohio. Indians and pioneers, forgotten since the original settlement of the county, are being recognized again in the new "Natives and Newcomers" Exhibit at Sauder Village. Established in 1850, Fulton was among the last counties formed in the last area of Ohio to be settled.

As part of the Great Black Swamp, the northwest portion of the state was often bypassed by water transport. The dense forest and mucky ground made farming and transportation all but impossible. The Native Americans driven from their earlier Ohio homelands were allowed to resettle in the Black Swamp region. Ottawa, Miami, and Potawatomi occupied the area until the 1838 accord with the government banished them farther west. Ottawa Chief Wauseon moved with his remaining people to Kansas; when he could not adjust to the new life, he died there at age forty-five. Settlers in his homeland honored him by naming their new town after him. Wauseon became the county seat in 1870. Wauseon also honors native son Barney Oldfield. The colorful auto-racing pioneer was the first man to break the one-minute-mile (1903) and broke or reset numerous early racing records. As a barnstormer driving "Blitzen Benz" or "The Green Dragon," Oldfield championed auto racing as a people's sport beyond the rich elite who owned the early cars.

Fulton was at the heart of the 1830's border dispute because the state line of the time ran through the center of the county. The Battle of Phillips Corner, also called the Toledo War, ensued when Michigan militia confronted the Ohio surveyors sent to re-mark the 1817 state line. The militia opened fire in the confusion, but there were no casualties. To resolve the conflict, Ohio retained Toledo and Michigan added the Upper Peninsula to its territory.

The first white settlers to brave the swamps were Amish-Mennonites. After arriving in 1834, they spent over ten years digging drainage ditches and clearing the forest. For the next one hundred plus years livestock and feed crop farms have sustained Fulton. Its established way of life, however, has not been without some frontier excitement. The town of Ai once had so many saloons that the citizens named it for the Biblical town that Joshua destroyed for its sin. It is the shortest-named town in Ohio.

Concerned for preserving the historic rural lifestyle of Ohio, philanthropist Erie J. Sauder built a village in 1976 to feature the farming and crafts of a bygone era. Sauder made his fortune with the Sauder Woodworking Company he founded in 1934. He gathered dozens of Great Black Swamp and other early buildings together north of Archbold. The old ways featured in Sauder Village attract thousands of new visitors to its living history. The newest exhibit shows the cooperative working and living between pioneers and Native Americans' –a new vision of old misconceptions.

Fulton County is named for artist, engineer, and builder Robert Fulton who is most remembered for perfecting the steamboat.

FULTON
WIGWAMS AT SAUDER VILLAGE

As I drove up through the northwest part of Ohio, I could imagine Indians moving north across the state's vast plains on their way to Canada, building temporary settlements of wigwams like these pictured. I was impressed by Sauder Village and their Native & Newcomers outdoor display. Light was dropping; it was cold and the paint stiffened, but not before getting a descent representation of the scene.

–Richard Canfield

Wigwams at Sauder Village   18" x 24"   Oil on Canvas - Richard Canfield

Gallia

2000 Population - 31,069
Land Area - 469 Sq. Mi.
Persons/Sq. Mi. - 66.3

Tall tales of Paul Bunyan, Pecos Bill, and Johnny Appleseed enliven the lore of America's founding and expansion. Some legends, sadly, concern huge con-games and swindles such as the sale of Florida swampland, and the promise of Gallipolis, Ohio, as the potential capital of the new United States.

In 1790, Scioto Company land agents plied Europe with tales of Eden-like Ohio. So persuasive were they, that over 500 upper class French displaced by their revolution paid to rebuild their lives on the bountiful, beautiful banks of the Ohio River. When they arrived they discovered that agent William Playfair had absconded with their money. Not only were the immigrants' deeds worthless, but also the country was total wilderness with hostile Indians. The government eventually tried to rectify the wrong and allocated 24,000 acres to the French emigres, and

soldiers from nearby Marietta built a blockhouse and cabins for the new arrivals. Many of the refugees returned to France or left for other established cities such as New Orleans and St. Louis, but over two hundred immigrants did settle on what is now Gallipolis City Park.

By 1807, only twenty families of the original group remained, but Gallipolis and Gallia County were firmly established. While the wilderness receded reluctantly, the town grew rapidly. Cushing Tavern, built in 1819, included a ballroom with the inn rooms and tavern. Cushing invited so many guests to "our house" that the sobriquet "Our House" remains today. Lafayette stayed there when he visited Gallipolis in 1825. The three-story Federal building was donated to the Ohio Historical Society in 1944 as a memorial to the French.

The river port thrived as a supply stop for settlers going west and north. Refugees from another minor scandal joined the French in 1818. A historical marker notes the landing site of a barge of Welsh that broke loose when their convoy stopped for supplies on the way to Butler County. The main party simply left their compatriots behind. The deserted group decided to stay and established a Welsh culture in southern Ohio that survives today, especially in their churches. The Tyn Rhos Congregation (1838) is open for special occasions and the Nebo

Congregation church (1854) still has Sunday and other special services.

During the heyday of Ohio River commerce, Gallipolis teemed with riverboats and dozens of steamboats crossing the river to Parkersburg daily or transporting goods and people further south. Commemorating this era, the steamboat "Chesapeake" moored there was honored on a US stamp in 1989.

Civic pride and hard work have turned challenges into opportunity in Gallia County. Other scandals that have inadvertently contributed to progress for Gallipolis included three burned courthouses. Convicted felons angry at their sentences burned down early buildings in 1858 and 1877. A third fire in 1961 led to temporary quarters until the current courthouse was built in the 1980's in the style of the 1879 building.

The Gallia County legacy of hospitality extended to many refugee groups. The County Children's Home is the longest standing in Ohio. Dr. Charles M. Holzer was world-renowned for his research and care of epileptics and his wife was equally noted for her nursing school. The hospital they built once had 100 buildings and over 3,000 residents. Today, the Holzer Medical Center honors Dr. and Mrs. Holzer for their work.

Rio Grande native Bob Evans and his family founded a restaurant chain that has spread across the U.S.

Gallia, land of the Gauls, takes its name from the ancient Romans' name for France.

GALLIA
"OUR HOUSE" TAVERN, GALLIPOLIS

I hate to say it, but I found the back of the tavern more interesting than the front (not that the front was not worthy of painting). I just liked how you could look down the alley and see the Ohio River in the distance, and the pattern of the light and dark shapes.

–Tom Harbrecht

"Our House" Tavern, Gallipolis, Ohio   18" x 24"   Oil on Canvas - Tom Harbrecht

Geauga

2000 Population - 90,895
Land Area - 404 Sq. Mi.
Persons/Sq. Mi. - 225.2

Connecticut Yankees bought land for 42 cents per acre in what was to become northeastern Ohio. They felt right at home when they arrived at the Connecticut Western Reserve, finding large stands of sugar maple trees and snow – lots of it. Geauga County was formed in 1806.

On a plateau 500 feet above Lake Erie, Geauga County buffers the moister air and cooler temperatures of the wind from the lake as it turns into snow. Surrounding counties also have "lake effect" snow, but Geauga consistently sets Ohio records by measuring its yearly averages in feet, not inches.

Geauga County's first settlers carried their New England tradition of maple syrup manufacturing into the county's abundant maple forests. While not as famous as New England maple products, Geauga County has led Ohio's production

and is a national leader as well.

There are no towns in Geauga County, only villages. Chardon was founded four years after the state legislature designated its wilderness locale to be the county seat. Other villages played prominent roles in county and state history as well. Burton is the center of the maple syrup industry. A sugar camp operates in the town square during the annual Maple Festival each Spring. Burton is also hometown to politicians Peter Hitchcock and Seabury Ford. Dubbed "Father of the Ohio Constitution," Hitchcock served as Ohio Supreme Court Justice for twenty-eight years. Ford was Governor 1849-51. More than twenty-two original Geauga structures built as early as 1798 have been brought from various sites to "Century Village" just south of Burton to display the Western Reserve heritage.

Thompson village claims "whiz kid" Charles M. Hall, who experimented in his woodshed as a teenager on ways to cheaply produce aluminum. After graduating from Oberlin College, he continued his successful pursuit and searched for investors. In spite of Hall's young age, Andrew Mellon believed in him and together they founded what became Aluminum Company of America (ALCOA).

Dairy farms have dominated agriculture in the county, especially in

cheese making. German Mennonites and Amish came to the area in the early 1800's and their traditional farming has prospered. Middlefield is one of the largest Amish communities in the world.

In contrast to the conservative culture of the Amish, Newbury and South Newbury were hotbeds of political action in nineteenth century Geauga County. The Union Chapel in South Newbury was nicknamed "The Free Speech Chapel" and "The Cradle of Women's Suffrage" for its role in the women's rights movement. Suffragettes who urged their cause at Union Chapel included Susan B. Anthony, Louisa May Alcott, and Lucy Stone. Ohio became the fifth state to ratify the Nineteenth Amendment on June 16, 1919. The Ohio Women's Suffrage Association called for a final pilgrimage to Newbury and to the Suffrage Oak, which had been planted to commemorate the US centennial, July 4, 1876. The women had used it as a symbol of the strength for their cause for over forty years.

Geauga is a Native American word meaning "raccoon."

GEAUGA
CHARDON IN WINTER

Chardon in Geauga County has been called the snow capital of Ohio. I visited this stately courthouse in Chardon on a partly sunny, yet very cold January day. The landscape was blessed with a generous supply of snow. Back in the studio, I took to the challenge of capturing the dancing lights in this otherwise cold, frosty winter wonderland.

–Mark Gingerich

Chardon in Winter   22" x 24"   Oil on Linen - Mark Gingerich

Greene

2000 Population - 147,886
Land Area - 415 Sq. Mi.
Persons/Sq. Mi. - 356.5

Eclectic describes Greene County from the days of the prehistoric Hopewells and Adenas through to the present farmers and academics. Greene's natural resources and human tolerance reflect the diversity the area has come to represent. Old Town, formerly Old Chillicothe, was a Shawnee village from approximately 1100 until they were driven out. John Wilson and his sons were the first white settlers, building cabins in Ferry. Tecumseh frequently visited the Galloway log cabin near Goes Station (1797). The still-intact cabin, moved several times, is now in Xenia, the county seat. Greene County became official in 1803.

The Little Miami River runs a rugged course through the county. Now a National Scenic River, it was originally home to dozens of mills along its banks. Clifton (1802) at the head of the falls at Clifton Gorge had as many as sixteen mills operating at one time, producing thousands of items for the War of 1812 and the Civil War. The Clifton Mill today is the largest water powered gristmill in the United States. The Gorge is adjacent to John Bryan State Park established in 1918 as a "... forestry, botanic and wildlife reserve and experiment station."

From the early 1800's, Yellow Springs was a health spa. Dr. and Mrs. Thomas Low Nichols arrived to start their Memnonia Institute in 1856, but struggled with town critics, notably Horace Mann, president of newly formed Antioch College, over morality issues of their free love philosophy. The Nichols enrolled only twenty students in their School of Health, Progress, and Harmony before all converted to Catholicism and left the area in 1857. Perhaps the curriculum with "vows of chastity, strict diet, and religious routine" did not meet the expectations of the enrollees.

Nearby Antioch, when it opened in 1853, welcomed women and blacks along with the men. Educational reformers Horace Mann and his equally zealous wife Mary were hired from Massachusetts to run the non-sectarian school. Mann's innovative curriculum stressed peace, added the sciences, and allowed women to study the same subjects as white men. Olympia Brown, an 1860 graduate, led the way in expanding even those liberal practices. She insisted on memorizing and delivering her papers as the men did; she wore the newly invented "bloomers" regularly and brought in prominent women speakers. Brown, a Universalist, was the first woman in America to be ordained from a "regular" theological program. Although experiencing some difficult times, Antioch has triumphed with its principles intact.

Also established in 1856, Wilberforce College is the nation's oldest private black university. The Cincinnati Conference of the Methodist Church closed its struggling school in 1862, but Bishop Daniel Payne of the African Methodist Episcopal Church raised enough money to buy it and became the first African-American to lead a university, 1863-1876. Wilberforce birthed Central State University, which became a separate institution in 1957.

In 1862 Moncure Daniel Conway brought former slaves from his family plantation to establish Conway Colony. A minister, Conway believed they would be accepted in Yellow Springs because it was known as a progressive village.

Xenia is best known for the 1974 tornado that devastated the town. The largest ever recorded in the United States, It did over $100 million damage.

Greene County was named for the noted Revolutionary War hero, General Nathaniel Greene.

GREENE
CLIFTON GORGE

Descending down the stairs to the riverside, we found a mystical wall of natural cliff in all of its damp grays, blues, and moss-covered dark greens, running alongside the river twenty yards from the river's edge. The variations of splotches of dried attachments removed by the climate from years ago left markings of calligraphic interest on the vast outreaches of stone, and varied growths from soft moss beds to ancient ferns and slender trees dressed up the crevasses. What a wonder of nature to be found so close to home — the natural home of which Mrs. English would tell me when I was 21 years old, "Oh, Kaye, when you see a natural splendor like that, could you disbelieve there is a higher deity?" We would walk on, admiring all that we found that day. That's the kind of day the Clifton Gorge was.

—Kaye Michele Darling

Clifton Gorge   24" x 18"   Oil on Canvas - Kaye Michele Darling

Guernsey

2000 Population - 40,792
Land Area - 522 Sq. Mi.
Persons/Sq. Mi. - 78.2

Stories intertwining folklore with facts make history. Stories of Native Americans and early white settlers abound in Guernsey County. They tell how surveyor Ebenezer Zane established Cambridge in 1796 on the site of a former Native American town as he was building Zane's Trace. That road and the later National Road (now U.S. 40), which followed the same path in Guernsey, opened up the West. The first bridge authorized in the Northwest Territory in 1801 crossed Wills Creek in Cambridge where Ezra Graham had a ferry service. The bridge was made from logs with a puncheon split log surface. When the National Road came through twenty years later, sturdier stone bridges took the place of ferries and fords. Five "S" bridges built on the National Road in Ohio were the latest in bridge technology. The "S" design enabled the bridge to be at right angles to the riverbed with curved approaches meeting it. Stories assert the reason for the "S" was to stop runaway horses.

Cambridge grew again in 1806 when a large band of immigrants from the Isle of Guernsey, England, encamped here. Legend insists that the women refused to proceed any farther, so the group stayed. Guernsey became a county in 1810 with Cambridge as the county seat. Pioneers of all sorts poured in for the promised opportunities. One strangely clad and fire-eyed Joseph Dilt, a fervent evangelist, gathered crowds of converts in 1828 when he proclaimed himself the Messiah. The "Leatherwood God" disappeared within a year, but left many believers.

Blacksmith William Reed served in the War of 1812 first under General William Henry Harrison then under Commodore Oliver Hazard Perry, when he ran short of navy men. Reed and other army men manned the cannons during the Battle of Lake Erie, so the sailors could maneuver the ships. He is one of those depicted in the painting at the Ohio Statehouse Rotunda that tells the story of battle.

Coal and glass making led Guernsey County industries in the Nineteenth Century. Guernsey was one of Ohio's leading coal producers late into the 1900's when the high sulpher coal became environmentally undesirable.

Cambridge became synonymous with fine glass, especially Cambridge and Degenhart companies. Both of those have closed but retain museums for admirers. Mosser Glass and Boyd's Crystal Art Glass continue the tradition.

Civil War tales of Ohio action involved over 2,000 men from Guernsey. The conflict also reached the county in 1863, when General James Shackleford confronted Morgan's 600 Confederate raiders at Old Mill Road. The three Reb's killed are buried in the cemetery there; eight others were captured. One story states that Winterset's Elias Tetirick buried his Abolitionist papers to save them from Morgan. The Raider's were close, but did not stop.

Stories continue today with the Living Word outdoor drama in Cambridge and the Ohio Hills Folk Festival in Quaker City. The festival has been a tradition since 1904 with earlier roots as far back as the 1874 County Fair.

Guernsey County is named for the large number of immigrants from the Isle of Guernsey in the English Channel who settled there.

GUERNSEY
EASTER SUNDAY AT THE "S" BRIDGE

Mention Guernsey County and history and the "S Bridge" is the first thing people talk about. It is just 2 miles off of the Quaker City exit on I-70. I was painting on location here on Easter morning. It was sunny and quiet, except for the traffic of I-70 behind me. As I was nearing the end of my "painting window," an Amish man pulling a wagon of children crossed the bridge, stopped, and lifted a little girl into his arms so she could see over the top of the bridge. This painting was a pleasure to work on.

–Debra Joyce Dawson

Easter Sunday at the "S" Bridge   16" x 20"   Oil on Canvas - Debra Joyce Dawson

Hamilton

2000 Population - 845,303
Land Area - 407 Sq. Mi.
Persons/Sq. Mi. - 2,075.1

Hamilton County started like much of pre-urban Ohio. Prehistoric Adena and Fort Ancient Indians gave way to modern tribes such as Miami and Chippewa, who gave way to pioneers from eastern U.S. states and European immigrants. The Ohio River, however, insured the rapid growth that made Hamilton and its Queen City, Cincinnati, unique and world-famous. The area's first settlement in 1788, Columbia, was on the current site of Lunken Airport. Within months of each other, Losantiville and Northbend also emerged. In 1795, when General St. Clair made Hamilton the second county in the Northwest Territory, he renamed Losantiville, Cincinnati, and made it the county seat.

Immigrants poured into the region via the Ohio River. Its first steamboat, the Orleans, arrived in Cincinnati in 1811. Mark Twain's "floating wedding cakes without the complications" are still a main attraction on the river with a huge festival "Tall Stacks" featuring paddle- and stern-wheelers each fall. Many of the first immigrants to arrive were German. Over half of the current population has German roots. In addition to the city's signature Fountain, and the Roebling suspension bridge, German heritage is evident with the brewing and pork packing industries that built the city. By the mid-1800's, the county had the largest industrial concentration in the nation. Perched between the livestock and feed supplies and U.S. consumers, Cincinnati gained the moniker "Porkopolis" which it holds to this day. Noted industrialists from Cincinnati included William Procter and James Gamble (soap), Charles L. Fleishmann (yeast), and Stearns and Foster (cotton and mattresses).

The crowded city suffered several disasters during its history. One of every fourteen people in Hamilton County died in the cholera epidemic of 1850, including Harriet Beecher Stowe's infant son. The nation's worst maritime disaster occurred in 1865 on the riverboat the "Sultana." Built in Cincinnati in 1852, the ship was returning 2,300 freed Union POW's when the boiler exploded. Seventeen hundred died, 791 of them from Ohio. Many floods, 1937 being among the worst, also devastated the county. From these tragedies came reform in building and sanitation codes and disaster relief.

Cincinnati encouraged cultural pursuits. Since forming Ohio's first symphony and oldest Choral Festival (1873), Cincinnati has been renowned for the arts. Sculptors Clement Barnhorn and Hiram Powers, artists Frank Duveneck, John Twachtman, Robert Duncanson, and Robert Henri called Cincinnati home. Journalism and literature have thrived producing William Maxwell, first territorial newspaper editor, publishers Adolph Ochs of the New York Times, and authors Harriet Beecher Stowe, Fannie Hurst, Joshua L. Liebman, Steven Birmingham and poet Phoebe Cary, among others. Film and television stars from Cincinnati include: Doris Day, Theda Bara, Steven Spielberg, Ted Turner, and Sarah Jessica Parker. In 1869, the Cincinnati Red Stockings (now known as the Reds) became the first professional baseball team in the country.

City benefactors established the nation's first municipal university, the University of Cincinnati, in 1858. Samuel Lewis, the educator who created the public school system, and Daniel C. Beard, founder of the Boy Scouts of America, were from Hamilton County. Native son scientists include Albert Sabin, who developed a polio vaccine, and chemist Alfred Springer. Three United States Presidents, William Henry Harrison, Benjamin Harrison, and William Howard Taft hailed from Hamilton County, along with numerous other politicians and public figures.

Hamilton County is named for Alexander Hamilton, first U.S. Treasury Secretary.

HAMILTON
CINCINNATI SKYLINE
AND THE ROEBLING BRIDGE

I painted the skyline, as seen from Covington, Kentucky, but I was torn for a while between this location and the fabulous Art Deco Union Terminal. It was 96 degrees when I first went to Cincinnati to look at my recommended sites, too hot and hazy to paint the city, so I decided to wait. I didn't get back until March. I spent the night in Cincinnati and worked on location two days in a row, making two paintings. When I first arrived, the skyline was fogged in, and I thought, "Wow! What a great painting for the project." By the time I got set up, the fog was gone. That's plen air painting for you!

–Debra Joyce Dawson

Cincinnati Skyline and the Roebling Bridge   16" x 20"   Oil on Canvas - Debra Joyce Dawson

Hancock

2000 Population - 71,295
Land Area - 531 Sq. Mi.
Persons/Sq. Mi. - 134.2

A stroll "Down by the Old Mill Stream" reveals as much about the Hancock County of yesterday as the Hancock County of today. Frenchman Jean Jacques Blanchard settled as a tradesman in 1769 among the area's Shawnee Indians. The Blanchard River carries his name. Songwriter Tell Taylor remembered its beauty and romance from his hometown when he wrote that beloved song in 1908. Today, the mill is gone, but running through Findley, the county seat, the Blanchard serves as a key to downtown restoration and is the heart of the county parks system.

The War of 1812 brought frontier strife as Colonel James Findlay opened a road to the river and built a stockade called Fort Findlay. When the War ended the Indians moved further west and settlement of the Great Black Swamp area to the north commenced. Hancock County was formed in 1820. One of Findlay's earliest industries was manufacturing equipment to drain the swamp so that land suitable for farming could be claimed from the fertile soil.

During the 1840's and 1850's an active Underground Railroad system worked in Hancock County, especially along what is now Route 68. Not only were many farmers involved, but townspeople were as well. An historical marker commemorates the spot where David Ada, a free African-American, had his barbershop and hid numerous fugitives in the Reed House. Aiding the Union cause, Findlay newspaperman David Ross Locke attacked slavery and the South with satiric letters to the editor under the pen name of Petroleum Vesuvius Nasby. President Lincoln liked the letters so well that wags said three things saved the Union – the army, the navy, and the Nasby letters.

When the Congressional Medal of Honor award was created in 1863, the first sixteen recipients were from Ohio. Two in the group in the "Great Locomotive Chase" were Hancock County natives William Bensinger and John R. Porter. All of the men were captured when the attempt to steal the Rebel engine "The General," failed. Porter escaped and Bensinger was part of a prisoner exchange a year later.

As the county grew so did its cultural institutions. The Churches of God, General Conference founded Findlay College in 1882. Today it is a thriving university, now joined by an Owens Community College (Toledo) branch and Southern Ohio College.

An oil and gas boom came to Hancock County in 1884. Hundreds of wells were drilled into the Great Lima Oil Field. The first practical use of natural gas in the mechanical arts developed here. 1887 brought 40,000 visitors to the area for the gas jubilee with Findlay streets ablaze with gas lights. The Ohio Oil Company, founded in 1887, when northwest Ohio was the world leader in oil production, was bought by Standard Oil Company in 1889, moved its headquarters from Lima to Findlay in 1905, and became independent again in 1911 when Standard Oil was broken up for antitrust violations. Ohio Oil became Marathon Oil in 1962, and was then purchased by United States Steel Corporation in 1986 before moving its headquarters to Houston, Texas in 1990. The esteemed Fostoria glassworks were among many companies that prospered during the long run of easily available gas and oil. Cooper Tire and Rubber Company continues to headquarter its worldwide operations in Findlay.

Hancock County was named after John Hancock, first signer of the Declaration of Independence.

HANCOCK
THE BLANCHARD RIVER

Late afternoon sun bathed the Blanchard River in greens and yellows. I was draw to the landing opening alive with the serenity and business of the lacy shapes and natural river reflections smiling back as the sun performed its magic descent behind the horizon.

–Kaye Michele Darling

The Blanchard River   16" x 20"   Oil on Canvas - Kaye Michele Darling

Hardin

2000 Population - 31,945
Land Area - 470 Sq. Mi.
Persons/Sq. Mi. - 67.9

Hogs and onions are two commodities with which Hardin began and continues to prosper. The northwest area of Ohio known as the "Great Black Swamp" was settled late not only because of the soggy terrain and dense forest, but also fierce fighting with the French, Indians, and finally the British. After the 1750's, the Shawnee and Wyandot tribes remained in the area allied with the British. As the Americans continued to push west, Duncan McArthur built a stockade at the Scioto River near Kenton in 1812. Fort McArthur guarded the supply route for the troops that finally vanquished the British and the Native Americans. Hardin became a county in 1820 with Kenton as its seat.

The important first step of county road building was Hull's Trail, built in 1812 to connect the Ohio Valley with Detroit. Outside Kenton, Pfeiffer Station

General Store continues to provide bulk items and Amish crafts in much the same way as when it was part of a stagecoach stop on the Sandusky Trail. The swamps produced Hardin's first market goods. Hog Creek Marsh was populated with wild swine. Although the marsh was drained in 1870, Hardin remains seventh in the state in hog raising. Likewise, the marshes yielded onions, for which the county became famous. Hardin County is eighty per cent agricultural to this day.

The Civil War took many of the area's men, but granted Hardin native Jacob Parrot the Nation's highest honor. Parrot was the first soldier awarded the Medal of Honor. He had joined Andrew's Raiders in the Great Locomotive Chase. Six of the men were captured and held until an 1863 prisoner exchange. As the youngest of the six, Parrot received the first medal from Secretary of War Stanton at the ceremony. The family treasured the award until they returned it to Congress in 1990. Parrot's Medal rests in an airtight case in the Capitol. Fort Kenton was a Civil War training camp in the 1860's, located on land of today's fairgrounds.

Prior to the Civil War the county was a rail center with Ada developing as it's hub. It operated a few lines until, in 1887, the Pennsylvania Railroad built a new depot larger and fancier than that day's standard. It serviced the system

between Crestline and Fort Wayne. The building had a telegraph office on the second floor. The town also burgeoned because of a new college.

Henry S Lehr, a Union veteran, opened the Northwest Ohio Normal Academy in Ada in 1871. A teacher, Lehr was appalled by lack of teacher training and began to hold classes during the summer in the Ada public school buildings. At first the college with its practical and affordable curriculum was non-sectarian. As it grew, however, the college added a law school and agricultural and pharmacy curricula that required financial support, so the Methodist church took it over in 1898. The school was renamed Ohio Northern University in 1904.

Wilson Sporting Goods has manufactured athletic equipment including footballs in Ada since 1913. The "Official ball of the NFL" game balls have been hand-made here since 1941. Another Hardin County sports attraction for forty-five years has been the Kenton Nationals, the largest coon dog field trials and water race in the world.

Hardin County was named for Colonel John Hardin. While he was on a peace mission in 1792, hostile Indians executed him.

HARDIN
PFEIFFER STATION GENERAL STORE

The Pfeiffer Station General Store was an early stagecoach stop that must have served the traveler well. Its aged surface and natural rustic setting afforded me wonderful contrasts and good light. Plus, an occasional tasty old-time snack break.

–Richard Canfield

Pfeiffer Station General Store   20" x 20"   Oil on Canvas - Richard Canfield

Harrison

2000 Population - 15,856
Land Area - 404 Sq. Mi.
Persons/Sq. Mi. - 39.3

Boom and bust cycles are historically common, but Harrison County has had highs and lows to the extreme. Throughout its periods of abundance and want, however, county history has been rich with noted people. Scotch-Irish immigrants from Pennsylvania settled the county, which was officially formed in 1813. Its seat is Cadiz.

Colleges founded early in the county's history did not survive financial problems, but each left a legacy. Scio College offered a unique program, the "One Study" system, where students took one course at a time. The College merged with Mt. Union in 1911. Franklin College in New Athens educated more Presbyterian ministers in the 1800's than any other college west of the Alleghenies. Illustrious alumni included George McCook (of the fighting McCooks), mathematician Joseph Ray, and statesman/judge John Bingham.

Franklin became part of Muskingum College in 1927. Hopedale Normal was Ohio's first teachers' college.

Sheep were the impetus of the county's first boom. By the end of the nineteenth century, Cadiz, was recognized as the richest town in America because of bank deposits from sheep farmers. An oil boom in Scio in the late nineteenth century resulted in temporary mayhem with as many as 1,500 derricks in the village at once. The late 1930's brought the short-lived prosperity again to Scio when L.P. Reese revived a defunct pottery. Coal fed a last Harrison County boom after WWII, until the coal's high-sulfur content and air pollution regulations put Ohio's entire coal mining industry into decline.

Matthew Simpson, born in Cadiz in 1811, was the well-known Methodist preacher who delivered Abraham Lincoln's eulogy. Lincoln admired John A. Bingham as an orator and statesman. He was the special Judge Advocate for the trial of Lincoln's assassins. Later, as a Supreme Court judge, he authored the Fourteenth Amendment and presided over the impeachment proceedings against President Andrew Johnson. New Rumley claims George Armstrong Custer, born in 1839. The youngest Union Civil War general at 23, he later led 264 men to their death against Chief Sitting Bull at the Battle of Little Bighorn in 1876.

Denton True "Cy" Young, born in Gilmore, pitched the first perfect game in the American League and won 511 games, more than any other pitcher. The Cy Young Award has honored Major League pitchers since 1956. Harrison County's Mary L. Jobe Akeley was an explorer honored for her 1920's work studying gorillas and advancing the emerging science of conservation in the Belgian Congo. Jacob Ebert of Cadiz received the first patent for a soda fountain in 1833.

One Harrison County native son stands out as favorite – Clark Gable, born in Cadiz in 1901. Gable's fans come to Cadiz in a steady stream. His original birthplace was torn down in the 1960's, but his popularity prompted a foundation in his name to rebuild a replica that opened 1998.

Harrison County was named after War of 1812 hero, General William Henry Harrison, who later was the ninth President of the U.S.

HARRISON
NOTTINGHAM
PRESBYTERIAN CHURCH

I was told it was one of the oldest Presbyterian churches in the county. On this late fall day, the colors had great range but had begun to lose some of the brightness. It was a challenge to try to capture the subtleties with such a colorful palette.

–Richard Canfield

Nottingham Presbyterian Church 18" x 24" Oil on Canvas - Richard Canfield

Henry

2000 Population - 29,210
Land Area - 416 Sq. Mi.
Persons/Sq. Mi. - 70.1

The famous lines "amber waves of grain" and "fruited plain" from America the Beautiful could have been written about Henry County. Over ninety percent of the land is farmland along the fertile Maumee River Valley. Henry has the third largest wheat crop in Ohio as well as significant acreage in truck farming. The county also has the world's largest Campbell Soup plant in Napoleon, and McClure is billed the "Radish Capital of the World." Today's immigrants come to Henry County at harvest time. The mostly Hispanic migrant workers return each summer, some for over twenty-five years, to bring in the earth's bounty. As a result of this annual influx, Henry is home to one of only two Migrant Rest Centers in the U.S. It now includes housing, employment training, agricultural education, and health services to help the migrants.

The first immigrants to Henry met very different conditions. Europeans glimpsed the Great Black Swamp when trading with several Native American tribes who used the area as hunting grounds. On Historic Driving Map Tour Day (October 6) visitors can see the old Ottawa hunting reservation where a tree hedge marks the reservation boundary–an area an Indian brave could encircle in one day. The County's first American settlers came to Prairie des Mascoutin (now Liberty Center) after 1812. Samuel Vance, brother of Ohio Governor James Vance, established a trading post there. The notorious Girty brothers switched allegiance after the Greenville Treaty and helped the British incite riots among the Indians against the American settlers. The brothers retreated to Girty's Island and Point about five miles upriver from Napoleon. George established a trading post but when the British abandoned the Girtys and left the area after the War of 1812, the traitorous brothers left, too.

Germans fleeing political unrest in their homeland arrived when the Miami-Erie Canal opened an otherwise impenetrable swampy forest. The first towns, Damascus and Flat Rock, were along the canal. From there, the newcomers cleared the land and drained the swamps to uncover the extremely fertile soil and gradually sowed the fields that created the modern landscape. Visible ditches along the fields still function. Henry County was chartered in 1820; Napoleon became the county seat in 1855.

The Ohio Bicentennial Barn project took over five years with artist Scott Hagan painting the logo on at least one barn in each of Ohio's eighty-eight counties. Each red, white, and blue logo takes about eighteen hours and seven gallons of paint to accomplish. The pictured barn opposite is on U.S. Route 6 east of Napoleon.

Three natural park areas in Henry County give glimpses of prehistoric Ohio: Meyerholtz Wildlife Park, Maumee State Forest, and the Mary Jane Thurston State Park. From Liberty Center west, ridges of sand or old beaches, called Oak Openings, exist from the time when the glaciers receded and created a Lake Erie much larger than it is today. Post-glacial dunes, bogs, prairies, and unique vegetation survive in these fragile preserves.

Henry County is named for Patrick Henry, Governor of Virginia, American Patriot, and celebrated Revolutionary orator.

HENRY
BICENTENNIAL BARN

I chose to do one of the 88 barns with the bicentennial logo to signify the different ways that people are commemorating our state's bicentennial.

–Richard Otten

Bicentennial Barn   18" x 24"   Oil on Canvas - Richard Otten

Highland

2000 Population - 40,875
Land Area - 553 Sq. Mi.
Persons/Sq. Mi. - 73.9

Highland County sits on the high land between the Little Miami and Scioto Rivers. The prehistoric Hopewell Indians made the area a hub of their culture between 100 B.C. and 500 A.D. Its mile-and-one-half-around earthworks make Fort Hill one of the best-preserved enclosures in North America. Later, the Shawnee made the area their home. The Seven Caves near Bainbridge are also rich in Native American history. Three state parks and a private nature sanctuary preserve the natural settings for posterity.

The stream in Rocky Fork State Park 12,000 years ago was blocked by a glacial remnant that so abruptly changed direction that it created its 75' gorge. In the early 1800's Rocky Fork gave early settlers swiftly running water for a number of mills. Paint Creek State Park lies at the Appalachian Plateau edge, the boundary between hilly and flat Ohio

regions. Pike Lake State Park began as a Civilian Conservation Corps project in the 1930's. The Highlands Nature Sanctuary strives to recreate the wilderness of Ohio. Settlers cleared the virgin forest that once covered the entire Northwest Territory in only twenty years. Few old-growth stands survive, but the Highlands Sanctuary organization is attempting to resurrect one in the Rocky Fork Gorge.

Additional parks include Paint Creek Park, which has Pioneer Village, a working replica of an early 1800's farm. The Lynchburg covered bridge, one of the few remaining in southern Ohio, sits next to Ruth Crampten Memorial Park.

An unusual natural event occurred near Princeton in 1893 when one of only two witnessed meteorite landings in Ohio was recorded. The meteorite that fell remained as a 1.98 pound rock.

Highland became a county in 1805. A committee chose Hillsboro with its seven hills as the ideal central location to be the county seat. The courthouse, built from 1832-34, is Ohio's oldest in continuous use.

Hillsboro was home to Eliza Jane Thompson, wife of Judge Thompson and daughter of Ohio Governor Allen Trimble. In 1873, Eliza and several other women actively responded to a temperance preacher. On Christmas Day over seventy-five women began visiting drugstores and saloons urging pledges

to quit serving alcohol. They got on their knees to pray and sing until the vendors acquiesced or left town. All, that is, except a Mr. Dunn who sued the women for obstructing his business and was awarded $5.00. This crusade was the forerunner of the Women's Christian Temperance Union, organized later in Cleveland. Ironically, when prohibition was repealed in 1934, the State of Ohio opened a liquor store on the site of Mr. Dunn's place.

Greenfield has a wonderful legacy in its school buildings. Industrialist Edward Lee McClain donated the high school to the town in 1914 complete with Greek and Roman sculpture and murals and paintings. The architecture and aesthetic setting became a national model for public school facilities. McClain later donated a vocational building complete with an indoor swimming pool, an athletic field and field house, cottages for the custodians, and a bus garage.

Highland County was named for its terrain.

Covered Bridge at Lynchburg   16" x 20"   Oil on Canvas - Mark Gingerich

Hocking

2000 Population - 28,241
Land Area - 423 Sq. Mi.
Persons/Sq. Mi. - 66.8

Hocking County has long been a destination for many. The Shawnee, Wyandot, and Mingo Native Americans hunted in the rugged hills using a common trail ending at Ash Cave. When white settlers found this immense recessed cave, they also found huge piles of ashes as large as 100' long by 30' high and 3' wide. The Indians presumably used the site for hundreds of years of campfires and perhaps some primitive smelting. Tar Hollow was a campground, too. Trails from the cave led to the salt licks further south.

Thomas Worthington laid out Logan, now the county seat, in 1816, as an investment to lure settlement. He built two mills on the Hocking River as added incentive and donated one of the town squares to be a market. Growth was slow but steady, and Hocking became a county in 1818. The market square continues

in use to this day.

The Hocking Canal system reached Logan in 1840 enabling exchange of goods and services from small farms, mining, and manufacturing. The remains of canal lock #12 are visible today. This Sheep Pen Lock really did hold sheep after the canals closed. Arrival of the railroads in the 1860's brought in more people to mine coal and salt as well as work at the mills.

The Hocking Valley and Hocking Hills have been tourist destinations since the mid-1800's, especially Ash and Old Man's Caves. The county claims more points of natural attraction than any other in Ohio. A substantial industry has grown around the scenic beauty of the area, drawing more and more people for longer and longer stays. The state began purchasing land as preserves in 1924. The Hocking Hills State Park and Forest now cover more than 11,000 acres.

Within the park breathtaking scenery and diverse wildlife are accessible to the thousands of annual visitors. Special destinations within the park include Ash Cave, Cantwell Cliffs, Cedar Falls, Conkle's Hollow, Old Man's Cave, and Rock House. Each locale has a storied history as well as breathtaking beauty. The most popular area is Old Man's Cave. Like Ash Cave, it is a huge recess in the cliff face. Hermit Richard Rowe moved here about 1796 and lived

in the cave until he died, hence the cave's name. Rowe is buried nearby. Conkle's Hollow is the deepest gorge in Ohio. W.J. Conkle, 1797, is carved in the sandstone of the west wall. Perhaps he was looking for the rumored Indian treasure that has never been found. Cedar Falls has the largest water volume as Queer Creek spills over the rock ledges. Rockhouse is the only true cave in the Park. A very early tourist attraction, in 1835 an entrepreneur built a hotel on the sight of the current shelter house. The cave was much lived in as it has natural carved windows and a water supply. Not only Indians lived there, but also adventurers, robbers, and bootleggers later utilized the rent-free space.

Close to the Park is Ohio's largest natural bridge. Rockbridge is 100' long and fifty feet high, with a 10-20 foot span. It is only accessible by canoe or hiking.

Hocking County's name is taken from the Indian word for the river, Hockhocking. It meant bottle-shaped.

HOCKING
BRIDGE AT OLD MAN'S CAVE

The grand specter of afternoon sun caught in the icy cave formations of Old Man's Cave was breathtaking in the winter cold. I loved the bridge set back against the warm yellow sky, still reflecting its glory on the darkening and frozen cave walls and ledges.

–Kaye Michele Darling

Bridge at Old Man's Cave   24" x 36"   Oil on Canvas - Kaye Michele Darling

Holmes

2000 Population - 38,943
Land Area - 423 Sq. Mi.
Persons/Sq. Mi. - 92.1

One wag asserts that Holmes County got a late start because the first settlers just came through on their way to being successful somewhere else. Few people stayed before 1800, but Mr.'s Miller and Johnson did create Millersburg in 1815. Dr. Robert Enos joined them and is credited with felling the first tree as well as organizing the town into the county seat. A remarkable man, Enos was Millersburg's first mayor and practiced medicine for over thirty years. His greatest achievement came in 1860 when as one of four delegates to the Chicago Republican convention, he early realized that Abraham Lincoln would come in two and one-half votes short of victory. Enos rallied some friends and Lincoln was nominated for President of the United States.

What makes Holmes unique is its lack of "progress." Thousands of tourists visit each year to witness what life may have been like for our ancestors in the "good old days." This very influx creates a precarious balance in the serene, picturesque area that could alter its character. Holmes County is the home to the largest population of Amish in the world. A group came from Pennsylvania in 1886, seeking new lands. Their agricultural husbandry and adherence to old ways, now for eight generations, have preserved a way of life the "English" have long forgotten.

While many Amish seek to avoid the modern sightseers, many of the more liberal sects have encouraged commerce. The area has been called Ohio's Switzerland because of the dairy farms and cheese making. The oldest business in Holmes is the Rastetter Woolen Mill near Berlin. It is the only woolen mill left in Ohio; they work the old-fashioned way. Wool is washed in rainwater, dried naturally, picked on a 100-year-old picking machine, and carded on the oldest continually operating carding machine in the U.S. Rastetter's superb work has been displayed in the Smithsonian. Other evidence of the hardworking, conservative lifestyle of the Amish and Mennonites is the abundance of carpentry and furniture making, much of it by hand in their homes as their custom dictates. Farmer's auctions in different towns occur weekly specializing in different goods from livestock to quilts. There are, of course, the horses and buggies. Seen especially early and late so the slower vehicles can avoid motor traffic, the buggies verify the simple, pacifist lifestyle of Amish. In Millersburg, the horses take precedence for parking–they get to park on the shady side of the courthouse.

Most of the sixty percent of Holmes population that is not Amish lives in the west part of the county. While the Amish usually keep to themselves, all residents share many commonalities and all strive to protect the land even though there is no zoning in the county. Winesburg is not the one from Sherwood Anderson's book, but the town folk were embarrassed when *Winesburg, Ohio* was first published; all seem to have adapted to the scandal it caused in 1919.

Holmes County was named for Major Andrew H. Holmes, who was killed during an unsuccessful attack on Fort Mackinac in 1814.

HOLMES
HOLMES COUNTY FIELDS

I was fortunate to come upon this Amish farmer one crisp spring morning as he was sowing the spring seed with his robust team of horses. I enjoyed watching man and beast work together in this rolling land.

– Mark Gingerich

Holmes County Fields   24" x 30"   Oil on Canvas - Mark Gingerich

Huron

2000 Population - 59,487
Land Area - 493 Sq. Mi.
Persons/Sq. Mi. - 120.7

Railroad trains crisscross Huron County over 100 times daily. The train whistle is music to the county's residents; it means jobs and prosperity for the farmers who make up eighty percent of the population.

The original residents were Native Americans. The Iroquois defeated the Erie Native Americans who resided in the area. Mingo, Seneca, and Wyandot followed into these hunting grounds before the white settlers pushed them west.

Huron originally was part of the Firelands of the Connecticut Western Reserve. During the summer of 1779, British troops attacked New Haven, New London, and Fairfield, Connecticut, and burned most of the towns leaving thousands homeless and jobless. At the end of the War the Connecticut legislature awarded the western portion of their reserve to the "Fire sufferers." Due to the time lag between claims and settlements, the heirs of the victims comprised most of the actual settlers. From that time the land was cleared and steadily farmed. Huron became a county in 1809.

Platt Benedict built the first house in Norwalk, the county seat, in 1815. When the Firelands and other New England immigrations slowed by 1828, the German influx continued to expand the farmland. A big early crop was celery; Huron has continued as a mixed growing region raising vegetables, fruit, and soybeans as well as supporting dairy farms.

The railroads dramatically altered the county. Bellevue became the rail and commercial hub of Huron and surrounding counties. In 1837, the Mad River and Lake Erie Railroad began service through what was then Amsden's Corners. Surveyor James Bell had taken a slightly circuitous route from Tiffin to Sandusky; hence Bellevue was born as the rail center.

President Lincoln's funeral train went through New London on its slow journey from Cleveland to Columbus in 1865. The rail companies built another rail center, Chicago or Chicago Junction, in 1871 with that Illinois city as its terminus. Willard became its name in 1917. Through additions and mergers, the rail traffic continues. The Mad River and NKP Railroad Society Museum in Bellevue tells the complete story. In the post-railroad heyday, few counties still thrive because of railroad activity. Huron does. The Norfolk Southern operates a rail car and locomotive repair center in Bellevue, and CSX has expanded its operations in Willard.

Railroads played a huge role in the success of Bellevue boy Henry Flagler (1830-1913). Flagler started The Standard Oil Company with John D. Rockefeller in 1870. The wealth Flagler accumulated was put to use in developing Florida's east coast. The towns of St. Augustine, Palm Beach, Fort Lauderdale, and Miami became playgrounds of the rich in large part due to Flagler's East Coast Railroad.

Huron County's most famous son, however, had nothing to do with farming or railroads. Paul Brown, Football Hall of Fame member, coached The Ohio State University to a national football championship in 1942, and organized and coached both the Cleveland Browns and the Cincinnati Bengals. He changed the way football was played and coached. He was the first coach to use classroom techniques, to call plays from the sidelines, and he invented the helmet face guard, among other innovations.

Huron County is the French name for the Wyandot Indians who lived in the area.

HURON
THIRD HORIZON

In this county, one is able to see vast distances because of the flat nature of the landscape, due to the glacier movement in this area. My painting focuses on how one travels through this staggard space, toward the distant horizon.

–Richard Otten

Third Horizon   20" x 30"   Oil on Canvas - Richard Otten

Jackson

2000 Population - 32,641
Land Area - 420 Sq. Mi.
Persons/Sq. Mi. - 77.7

Salt. Life-giving salt brought animals. Life-giving salt brought hunters. Life-giving salt, finally, brought settlers. Salt brought prosperity. Jackson County chartered in 1816, grew from this precious resource.

Signs of the earliest humans are startling. Prehistoric Fort Ancient or the Hopewell Indians were here around 1000-1650 A.D. They carved in sandstone over 35 distinct birds, reptile and other animal images seen today at the Leo Petroglyph. The Shawnee and other historic tribes used the salt springs for hundreds of years. They used prisoners/slaves for the hard labor of boiling and extracting the salt. Legend includes Daniel Boone among the captives that toiled here at one time. Whites began their salt trade in 1798 with the "Old Scioto Salt Works." Salt was so important that the U.S. government

granted the State of Ohio use of a six-square-mile area for the production and sale of the salt, then in 1824 allowed them to sell the land when better sources were located. Terms of the sale limited proceeds to "literary purposes."

Abolitionist "Big" George L. Crookham established a school in 1836. Short-lived, pro-slavery neighbors burned it down. His legacy, however, continued through his student John Wesley Powell who saved Crookham's work on salt licks' history. Powell went on as a geologist to lead Western expeditions as far as the Grand Canyon and the Columbia River. He later organized the U.S. Geological Survey and was its first director. Today a monument stands for him in Jackson City.

Jackson County's next growth burst also resulted from capitalizing area natural resources when the many Welsh settlers began mining. Abundant wood for charcoal joined with iron ore and coal to fuel a large iron industry. By the Civil War Ohio was the nation's leading iron center. The iron for the Monitor, which repelled the Merrimack in their famous sea battle in the mouth of the Chesapeake, came from the Jefferson furnace near Oak Hill, as did much of the ordnance in the U.S. arsenal at Harper's Ferry. Buckeye Furnace (1852-94) has been reconstructed around the original chimneystack, so Jackson's iron legacy remains visible. Visitors can see the

charcoal-fired blast furnace, the casting shed, and the charging loft where iron ore, limestone, and coal were loaded into the furnace. Nearby is the company store. The big coal find in 1869 continued local prosperity. Harvey Wells founded Wellston that became famed for the best bituminous coal in the world. By World War I natural resources dwindled and the industry declined.

Left with mined-out but cleared land, Jackson County once again prospered from nature. Apple orchards now soften the landscape and provide strength in the more diverse economy. The apple's impact has been celebrated for over sixty years with the annual Apple Festival.

Jackson County also celebrates it famous son, James A. Rhodes, born in Coalton. Although he moved to Columbus early in his political life, he never forgot his roots. Through four four-year terms he served longer as Ohio governor than any other person.

The county is named for Andrew Jackson, famed War of 1812 hero.

JACKSON BUCKEYE FURNACE

My focus for the Buckeye Furnace in Jackson County was on the immensity of the structure. Built into the side of a hill, the furnace stands 50 feet over ground level. Along with the sheer mass of the building, I was interested in capturing the dynamic architecture of the structure.

–Richard Otten

Buckeye Furnace   24" x 30"   Oil on Canvas - Richard Otten

Jefferson

2000 Population - 73,894
Land Area - 410 Sq. Mi.
Persons/Sq. Mi. - 180.4

Those who wish to learn the history of Jefferson County need only visit the county seat, Steubenville, and study the more than twenty murals gracing various city walls that provide a comprehensive historic tour. In 1986, city leaders commissioned the paintings to encourage visitors to the aging town.

George Washington was one of the first explorers in the county when he camped at Mingo town, now Mingo Junction, during a surveying trip in 1770. The site was home to a mixture of eastern Indians on their way west. Among them was Chief Logan. He was a friend to white hunters and settlers, and remained neutral during much of the frontier fighting because of these friendships. The respect was mutual until for unknown reasons soldiers killed his entire family. The murderers were brought to trial, but acquitted.

Logan then made revenge on the white men his life's work.

Mingo Junction has a very different legacy today as part of the entertainment industry. The town has served as sets in such films as "The Deerhunter" (1978) and "Vision Quest" (1985). Actor Robert Urich hailed from Mingo Junction.

Fort Steuben was erected in 1786 to protect and house surveyors mapping out the newly available Northwest Territory lands. A settlement, LaBelle, grew outside the walls around the survey offices. When the task was completed, the officials deserted the fort, which burned down in 1794. The county formed in 1797 with LaBelle, renamed Steubenville, as its seat. The county has built a replica of the survey office in downtown Steubenville. The logs from the original land office were dismantled and rebuilt in its restoration.

Quakers were an important presence in Jefferson County from their arrival in 1803. Centered in Mt. Pleasant, they built a huge Meeting House. It held 2,000 people in 1814 during the first Annual Meeting west of the Alleghenies. It was used regularly until 1909. Mt. Pleasant was a major hub for the abolitionist movement as well as an important Underground Railroad stop. From this town came one of the earliest influential papers, "The Philanthropist." Ohio's first abolitionist convention was held at the Meeting House in 1837.

Jefferson County was a river port and passage to the west until the first steel mill opened in 1856 and brought an increased population. The steel industry dominated both sides of the Ohio River for more than a century. Coal mining in eastern Ohio fueled industrial growth as well. From the steel mills came Stuebenville's favorite son Dean Martin. Others notable show people from the county were Lillian Gish and Bobby Clark. Roy Plunkett invented Teflon.

The High Shaft deep underground mine, where workers dug two and one-half miles under the surface, had its heyday with war production in the 1940's. The mural on the Steubenville Ribor Building commemorates the famous mine, which closed in 1964.

Jefferson County took its name from Thomas Jefferson who was Vice President at the time of the county's founding.

JEFFERSON
FIRST FEDERAL LAND OFFICE

It took me quite a while to make contact with Jefferson County, but when I finally met with the folks there, they were really great. What a tour they gave me of their historic sites! It was difficult to choose, but I felt that the Land Office was the most significant of the sites I saw because it was the first stop one had to make if you wanted to buy a piece of the land and move "west." This log cabin, with all its original logs, has been moved four times. It now has a permanent home not too far from its original site. Thanks to Eleanor Naylor, Charles Green, Bill Croskey and Richard Delatori for all of their help and kindness.

–Debra Joyce Dawson

First Federal Land Office   16" x 20"   Oil on Canvas - Debra Joyce Dawson

Knox

2000 Population - 54,500
Land Area - 527 Sq. Mi.
Persons/Sq. Mi. - 103.4

Knox County not only has the mid-state location it shares with several other counties, it also has the center of it all–Centerburg. A boulder there proclaims the geographical center of Ohio. Settled by squatters who came over the mountains from Virginia and Maryland, Knox became a county in 1808. Mt. Vernon edged out its nearby competition, Clinton, for county seat with some questionable public relations moves involving Mt. Vernon folks acting as drunks in Clinton to discourage the Columbus entourage. Mt. Vernon thrived, Clinton disappeared.

One early pioneer who influenced the growth of the county was John Chapman, aka Johnny Appleseed. He visited often and owned two lots in Mt. Vernon. On the night of August 9, 1813, Chapman heroically ran from Mansfield to Mt. Vernon and back to get reinforcements for an impending Indian attack. Markers in both towns honor his valor.

The center of economic life in Knox County has been the Cooper Manufacturing Company. Started in 1835, Cooper perfected the steam-driven thresher that significantly increased farm efficiency. They later made several other farm machines before switching to locomotive engines and generators. Now a subsidiary of Rolls Royce, the company produces large compressors to push natural gas through pipelines.

Mt. Vernon banker Henry Curtis persuaded Philander Chase, Ohio's first Episcopal Bishop, to relocate his college from Worthington to Knox County. Chase was unhappy with the city temptations in Worthington luring his seminary students away from proper study. After hiking through the hills in 1824, Chase settled on a spot for the new college and cultural center of Knox County. A Celtic cross marks the spot where Chase stopped and proclaimed, "This will do." The Bishop had raised funds in England for the Episcopal institution from Lords Kenyon and Gambier. He promptly named the college Kenyon and its town Gambier. Murals in the town post office recall these events. Enamored with Gothic architecture, Chase brought stonecutters from England to build the impressive first building. Work started so soon after the War of 1812 that rumors surrounding the venture suggested that these Englishmen were building a fort. Fortress of learning would be more accurate. Kenyon has produced many illustrious alumni, including President Rutherford B. Hayes, Edwin Stanton, poet Robert Lowell, novelist E. L. Doctorow, and actor Paul Newman.

Mt. Vernon has a long history of supporting entertainment in a variety of ways. The Woodward Opera House (1851) is the oldest authentic Nineteenth Century theater in America. Among its performers was native songwriter Daniel Emmett who wrote "Turkey in the Straw," "Blue Tail Fly," and "Dixie" for minstrel shows he had originated. While these songs and others were extremely popular (even Lincoln liked "Dixie"), lax copyright laws left Emmett poor when he died in 1904. Hiram and Barney Davis, Knox County dwarfs entertained sideshows as "The Wild Men of Borneo" in the late 1800's. Comedian Paul Lynde hailed from Knox and Jonathan Winters attended Kenyon. A Mt. Vernon native, William Semple, invented one of the unsung joys of personal entertainment, chewing gum, in 1869. By patenting sweetened chiclets Semple perfected the idea from Indians who chewed spruce gum.

Knox County is named for General Henry Knox, first U.S. Secretary of War.

KNOX
OLD KENYON

I have a real affinity for Kenyon College. Not too long after arriving in Columbus, business took me to the quaint little town of Gambier and the campus of Kenyon, where I made friends and wonderful memories of days rambling around marvelous old architecture like Old Kenyon. God blessed the day I was there with good light. It was serendipitous that I chose the angle I did. Supposedly, Chase stood at the sight of the Celtic Cross when deciding to build it in 1827.

–Richard Canfield

Old Kenyon 18" x 24" Oil on Canvas - Richard Canfield

Lake

2000 Population - 227,511
Land Area - 228 Sq. Mi.
Persons/Sq. Mi. - 996.9

Lake County may be the smallest in land area in Ohio, but its rank in size has a caveat. When the county was formed in 1840, it did not meet the minimum size the state required, so Lake was extended to the Canadian border. Three-quarters of Lake County is under water. What is above water on the thirty-one miles of shoreline is being held for posterity in spite of urban encroachment. Of the eight counties on Ohio's North Shore, the smallest is the biggest in preserving our Lake Erie heritage. The eleven parks in the county give us views into life here before the area was settled.

Lake County's first settler was Charles Parker at Hopkins Point/Mentor Marsh. The Marsh rests on an ancient channel of the Grand River. Among the rare and endangered species growing there are numerous reed grasses in the largest Phragmites marsh in Ohio. Mentor Lagoons Nature Preserve and Marina includes riverine marsh and the biggest unbroken bluff forest in Ohio. The first white settlers farmed the county, which quickly became heavily covered with nursery businesses. By the end of the 1800's, Mentor became known for its roses. Lawnfield in Mentor was the home of James A. Garfield while he served in the U. S. Congress. He was elected the 20th President, but served only four months before being assassinated in 1881. Garfield's family lived on there before it became a museum.

The Fairport Harbor is so-named because it is accessible when most of the other ports close. First Finns and Hungarians, then Slovaks immigrated here to fish. Later, they loaded by hand the huge amounts of iron ore sent from the harbor. The lighthouse on the breakwater pier replaced the one pictured in 1925, which is now the Maritime Museum and Lighthouse. Built in 1871, the current 60' high stone edifice replaced the original from 1825. Nearby Headlands Beach State Park and Dunes has a one-mile beach, the longest in the State. Naturalists are hoping the fragile dune ecology will make a comeback here after being nearly destroyed by development.

Two natural areas along the Chagrin River are also important. The Hach-Otis State Nature Preserve has been a bird sanctuary since 1944. Its steep cliff and bluff-top forest harbor bank swallows and kingfishers among a wide range of plants and animals. The Chagrin River Harbor also has steep walls of shale and a diversity of wildlife.

The county seat Painesville is somewhat inland, but has a natural phenomenon of its own. Little Mountain south of town is one of the highest points in the Western Reserve.

Also inland from the Lake is Kirtland. Local religious leader Sidney Rigdon persuaded Mormon founder Joseph Smith to come to Ohio to evangelize. Smith envisioned a temple for the followers. The first Mormon Temple opened in Kirtland in 1833, and the town prospered. As the Church grew, so did financial problems. When the bank owned by the Church failed, Joseph Smith and his followers were forced to leave town under cover of darkness. Pursuers chased them over two hundred miles into Illinois. The Kirtland Temple still stands as an architectural and religious shrine.

Lake County takes it name from its location on Lake Erie.

LAKE
LIGHTHOUSE

Being an ex-Navy man, I had to paint the lighthouse. It sits on a bluff overlooking the harbor. It was a very strong image.

–Tom Harbrecht

Fairport Harbor Light House   18" x 24"   Oil on Canvas - Tom Harbrecht

Lawrence

2000 Population - 62,319
Land Area - 455 Sq. Mi.
Persons/Sq. Mi. - 137.0

Ironton, the county seat of Lawrence, identifies what is most famous about the area – tons of iron. John Means built the first charcoal iron furnace, Union, in 1826. Ironmaster John Campbell founded Ironton in 1849 when he built furnaces there. Campbell and a partner had built the Olive Furnace in 1846. It was unique because its crucible was carved from solid rock and its burden path was a Roman arch over the pathway between the stockyard and the furnace. Each furnace fostered an entire community around it, and included clearing several hundred acres of forest for fuel, the foundry, houses, and all the auxiliary services that the workers needed. Olive Furnace church still stands, and the cemetery is still in use.

At their height, over half of the Hanging Rock Iron Region furnaces were in Lawrence County. The region took its name from a pioneer landmark in the County – the 400-foot sandstone cliff overhanging the Ohio River – and encompassed several Ohio and Kentucky counties rich in coal, iron ore, and forests.

The most colorful ironmaster was Nanny Scott Honshell Kelly, the only female ironmaster in the country, perhaps the world. Well-educated, Kelly traveled abroad, even meeting the Queen of England. She had taken over the Senter furnace when her husband died. Not only did she make a fortune, but she kept her furnaces going when the industry started to decline at the end of the century. She then stock piled iron and made another fortune by selling it in the early days of World War I. By all accounts Kelly was as good in the "feminine arts" as she was at business. She entertained frequently, was an art patron, built several mansions, and lived an enviable life. Sadly, her fortunes dwindled with the county's after World War I, and she died in her nineties dependent on relatives' support.

The iron industry disappeared gradually as the forests were depleted and higher grade ores began coming from other locales. Ironically, over half of the county is now the Wayne National Forest. In 1933, the Soil Conservation and Reforestation Corps replanted the hills around Vesuvius Furnace. The heavy forests that brought industry to the area have been replaced with forests that bring hikers and campers.

Some Lawrence County land remained as farmland. Proctorville farmer Joe Gillette planted apple orchards. In 1816, he gave his son Alanson a seedling that did not look as promising as the others to plant nearer the river. Several years later the neglected tree had produced numerous wonderful large red apples. The Gillettes named it Rome Beauty for their township, and it remains one of the most popular all-purpose apples.

Lawrence County is the southernmost in Ohio. South Point commands a view of Ohio, West Virginia, and Kentucky from the confluence of the Big Sandy and Ohio Rivers. While the town itself was not a steamboat center, most owners, pilots, and engineers on the river in the late 1800's were from South Point and the rest of Lawrence County, controlling up to seventy-five percent of the river traffic between 1860 and 1880. Lawrence currently is taking the lead in reviving this tri-state area as a major economic force.

Lawrence County took its name from navy officer James Lawrence, a War of 1812 hero, whose dying words were "Don't give up the ship!" Burlington, the county seat until 1852, was named after his hometown in New Jersey.

LAWRENCE "OLIVE" BLAST FURNACE

An evening drive leaving Lawrence with field studies of two historical places, and we stopped awestruck at the sight of "Olive," a blast furnace. She sat there taking up the entire forest area around her as if she dared someone to rest in her space. She appeared to be a giant primitive living area for a tribal group. But, of course, after we settled in and I painted the exploration around Olive and into her cavernous mouth explained part of her history. A wonderful goodbye to Lawrence County for the weekend of historical insight. Much more painting to do in Lawrence!

–Kaye Michele Darling

"Olive" 24" x 36" Oil on Canvas - Kaye Michele Darling

Licking

2000 Population - 145,491
Land Area - 686 Sq. Mi.
Persons/Sq. Mi. - 211.9

Ohio is a major crossroads of the United States; parts of Ohio have been crossroads since before recorded history. Licking County is one such area. Prehistoric Native Americans left clues that the area was not only the crossroads of a vast trading network stretching from Kansas to the Atlantic, from Michigan to Florida, but also the center of their ceremonial culture. As the largest system of geometric mound works anywhere in the world, the combined Octagon and Great Circle mounds in Newark along with the alligator effigy and nearby Wright Earthworks have intrigued and impressed Ohioans for 2000 years. Some evidence suggests that the Octagon serves an astrological/time function because it fits the nineteen-year lunar cycle. Native Americans still hail the monuments as sacred ground. As a cultural crossroads, much of the mounds now serve contemporary central Ohioans as a golf course.

For Shawnees, Wyandot, and other historic Indian tribes in the Licking River Valley two crucial commodities ensured the important trading route – flint and salt. The high-quality flint was famous across the eastern continent for tools and, especially, weapons. Flint outcroppings and Indian mining pits can still be seen at Flint Ridge State Memorial, run by the Ohio Historical Society. Salt licks brought game to be hunted, including bison. Small animal pelts provided the materials for trade and allowed early white settlers to develop a healthy industry making hats. This enterprise lasted until cheaper hats were imported from New York. Salt was mined and exported as well. The largest rabbit warren in the state in the mid-1800's was west of Newark.

Licking County became official in 1808. The location again became an important transportation crossroads when the National Road cut through the county in the early 1800's. The advent of the Ohio and Erie Canal heightened that role. Construction on the system began near Heath at the Licking summit in 1825. New York's Governor DeWitt Clinton ceremoniously dug the first spade full of earth for the canal, thus joining Ohio's two main trade and travel arteries. Railroads also criss-crossed the county linking manufacturers and farmers to markets all over America.

Race and gender lines have crossed among Licking County citizens, too. Abolitionist and Suffragette causes both found support here. Newark's Edward James Roy left to become the fifth president of Liberia. Victoria Clalfin Woodhull of Homer was the first woman candidate for President in 1872. She ran with Frederick Douglas her Vice-President as her People's Party nominee on a platform of women's equality in all respects, including free love. Woodhull was also the first female stockbroker in America. The nation's first woman bank cashier was Cora B. Clark of Utica, and she rose to be the first female bank president.

The conjunction of silica and natural gas in the area made perfect conditions for glass making as a major industry. The Heisey Glass Company had a worldwide market for their tableware glass until the 1950's. Utica had five companies specializing in hand-blown glass during the gas boom of the early Twentieth Century. They were known for window and cathedral glass until the boom ended in the Depression.

Licking County, Pataskala to Native Americans, was called that from the salt licks. It was also the pioneers' name for the river running through the county.

LICKING
SUNSET AT OCTAGON
EARTHWORKS, NEWARK

I live in Licking County, and I knew I wanted to paint something to do with the Native-American history there. In July 2002, I went to Flint Ridge, a neutral zone where native tribes from all over the east coast would gather flint for tools. I feel and cut my leg on the flint chips and found out first-hand why flint made such a great tool! But I wasn't happy with my painting so, one February evening, I went out to Octagon Earthworks in Newark. The mounds of this lunar calendar were covered in snow; everything was quiet; I was all along and painting in the cold as the sun was setting. Thanks to site manager Jim Kingery for a few good laughs over the phone and for helping me to understand the purpose and importance of this ancient place.

–Debra Joyce Dawson

Sunset at Octagon Earthworks   20" x 16"   Oil on Canvas - Debra Joyce Dawson

Logan

2000 Population - 46,005
Land Area - 458 Sq. Mi.
Persons/Sq. Mi. - 100.4

Logan became an Ohio county in 1817 following an influx of settlers. This was only the most recent wave in area settlement over the eons. Evidence suggests that at least three distinct groups of prehistoric Indians lived here, as did many modern tribes such as the Miami, Shawnee, Huron, Wyandot, and Delaware. Many existing towns in Logan County are on the site of the 12-15 Indian towns not vacated until the white settlers forced them out. A Native American presence DOES still exist in Logan County. The Shawnee Nation United Remnant Band owns the Zane Caverns near Zanesfield. In addition to offering unique cavern tours to the public, they share their heritage at the site.

An important Shawnee settlement, Blue Jacket's Town, became the county seat, Bellefontaine. Blue Jacket was a white man, Marmaduke Swearingen, captured in Pennsylvania as a small child. He was released back to the American's in a prisoner exchange, but as an adult chose to return to his adopted tribe. Blue Jacket married the chief's daughter and became a war chief himself. He led the "Seven Nations" to defeat in the Battle of Fallen Timbers and was key in the Treaty of Greenville.

Zanesfield reveals a similar story. Raised by the Wyandot tribe, Isaac Zane built the town on a former Indian town site and married a Wyandot Indian chief's daughter Myeerah. He became Chief White Eagle. Today's State Route 10 follows the Myeerah Trail, the old path between Zanesfield and Blue Jacket Town.

Continuing as a transportation center, Logan County was home to a settlement of slave descendents who may have been Underground Railroad "passengers." The one room schoolhouse they built in 1868 was in use until 1923. After years of neglect, in 1999 the Historical Society moved The Flatwoods School House to Veterans Park where it is a living history museum. The Quaker presence was also important in the area. They helped over 12,000 fugitive slaves through the area. The Goshen Friends Church (1807) was one of the stops. Many caves and rock formations were nearby hiding places.

Logan County's hub position was further solidified during the canal era. Miami/Maumee canal engineers built the Lewistown Reservoir from several small local lakes. The feat took six years (1851-57) and fed water to the canals until 1899. Renamed Indian Lake, the second largest man-made lake in Ohio has been a recreational waterway for more than a century.

The first railroad reached Bellefontaine in 1837. By the 1920's every major eastern railroad stopped in Bellefontaine, which had up to fifty-six trains per day. The roundhouse and switching yard gave service until 1980. Logan County had a major role in the transition as the rail industry gave way to the highways. The first concrete street in America was built in Bellefontaine in 1891 by George W. Bartholomew as a demonstration for his Portland cement. It amazed engineers all over; a block of it was exhibited at the 1893 Chicago World's Fair. Renovated only once, it is still in use. Bellefontaine also claims the world's shortest street, thirty–foot long McKinley Street.

Campbell Hill, at 1,550 feet, is not only the highest spot in Ohio but also between the Allegheney and Rocky Mountains. From 1951-1969, the North American Air Defense Command operated the 664th Aircraft Control and Warning Squadron station on this summit. Now the converted facility is the Ohio Hi-Point Career Center.

Logan County is named for General Benjamin Logan. He secured the county for white settlers when he destroyed Shawnee Villages there in 1796.

LOGAN
ZANESFIELD, MAD RIVER VALLEY

This is a view of Zanesfield, Ohio, hidden in trees, along County Road 10, looking down into the Mad River Valley. I liked the topography of the valley with the patchwork of fields and trees. The Myeerah Trail was an Indian trail that linked Zanestown (Zanesfield) to Blue Jackets Town (Bellefontaine). County Road 10 runs along the same path as the trail.

–Tom Harbrecht

Zanesfield, Mad River Valley   24" x 36"   Oil on Canvas - Tom Harbrecht

Lorain

2000 Population - 284,664
Land Area - 492 Sq. Mi.
Persons/Sq. Mi. - 578.0

If Ohio were called the Abolition State, then Lorain County's Oberlin would be the capital. Although the county erected a monument to John Frederick Oberlin in 1994, the legacy of those who originated and set the course for the College and town is as enduring.

When Nathan Perry set up his trading post in 1807 at the mouth of the Black River on Lake Erie, he could hardly have predicted the anti-slavery role the county would have. Lorain's location on the Lake was ideal for an important port, and that is, indeed, what developed. Fishing and shipbuilding were the earliest industries in both Lorain City and Vermilion. In the 1840's, when quarrying sandstone became big business in Amherst, the harbor shipped the product making the sandstone world famous, especially for grindstones. Amherst sandstone not only makes up the lake sea walls, it has

been used on buildings as disparate as Ottawa, Canada's Parliament buildings and the Hockey Hall of Fame. Though shipbuilding waned as Lake Erie business did, Lorain has revived its early industry with pleasure boating and fishing and now has the world's largest freshwater dry dock.

Shortly after Lorain became a county in 1824, Philo Stewart and the Reverend John J. Shippert founded Oberlin in 1833. Progressive from the start, Oberlin was the first college to admit women and African Americans. The Oberlin Conservatory of Music is also the first in the U.S. The town and the college have been intertwined ever since. First Church (1842) was the meeting site of the Oberlin Anti-Slavery Society. Memorial services were held here for John Brown's raid participants. Prominent abolitionist and Oberlin trustee Jabez Burrell not only helped slaves in Ohio make their way to freedom; he also funded the Selma, Alabama, freedman's school.

In 1858, runaway slave John Price was taken from his Oberlin "Underground Railroad stop" to Wellington by bounty hunters. Oberlin citizens marched there and blocked entrance to the hotel where Price was being held, then stormed the building to free him. Thirty-seven rescuers were indicted for breaking the law, twenty of those went to jail. Eventually, all were

acquitted. Underground Railroad stops were also in Huntington, Elyria, and Sheffield.

Many prominent Oberlin graduates have gone on to serve Ohio and the world. In 1850, Lucy Sessions was the first Black woman in the U.S. to earn a degree. John Mercer Langston was the first African-American to pass the bar in Ohio (1854) and the first to be elected to government office (1855) before going on to be professor, dean, and president of Howard University. After leaving there, he became Virginia's first Black congressman. General Giles Waldo Shurtleff served as commander of the first Black regiment in Ohio. Carl T. Rowan was the "Crusading Columnist" in the second half of the 20th Century. The Heisman Trophy is named for John Heisman whose inaugural, undefeated coaching season at Oberlin was the springboard that made him a pioneer of modern football.

Nobel Prize for Literature winner Toni Morrison grew up in Lorain. Archibald Willard is Wellington's pride. An original of his "Spirit of '76" hangs with other paintings in the museum there. The town has also honored him with a memorial in the town square.

Lorain is the Americanized version of the Lorraine Province in France.

LORAIN
WELLINGTON TOWNE HALL

I was attracted to three different sites in Lorain County: a waterfall, a draw bridge, but somehow, I just liked the look of the top of the town hall shining in the afternoon sun.

–Debra Joyce Dawson

Wellington Towne Hall   20" x 24"   Oil on Canvas - Debra Joyce Dawson

Lucas

2000 Population - 455,054
Land Area - 340 Sq. Mi.
Persons/Sq. Mi. - 1,336.6

Lucas County was born in and has flourished in a continuous state of ups and downs, conflict and stability. The ancient seas and glaciers shaped the land, and then receded. Native Americans hunted and fished along the shore and in the marshes, but could not hold the land by war or by treaty. Miami Chief Little Turtle and Shawnee Chief Blue Jacket rebuffed U. S. Generals Harmer and St. Clair, but retreated from "Mad" Anthony Wayne in 1794 when the Indians' British allies ignored the Battle of Fallen Timbers. Not until after the War of 1812 was Ohio safe for settlers. All except Lucas County. A border dispute with Michigan concluded with Lucas County boundaries set after the bloodless Toledo War in 1836.

The Great Black Swamp still blocked the way of county progress. So many frogs covered the marshes that Toledo has had the nickname, "Frogtown,"

for centuries. The present courthouse, built in 1897, has frogs on its outside trim.

Small settlements in the few land areas of the swamp began to grow slowly. The horse-powered Erie and Kalamazoo, the first railroad west of the Alleghenies and first to cross state lines, trotted from Toledo to Adrian, Michigan, by 1836. Real prosperity came to Lucas County when the Miami-Erie Canal opened with its terminus in Toledo. Previously roadless, Toledo had been virtually isolated from the state. Now the county not only had access to resources, but also could export products.

The Lucas County silica was of such high quality and fuel was so cheap that Edward Libby brought his glass company to Toledo from Massachusetts in 1883. Michael Owens brought his semi-automatic glass blowing equipment to the company in 1888; Toledo became the "Glass Capital of the World." When the demand for blown glass waned, they produced sheet glass and merged with Ford Plate Glass to become Libby, Owens, Ford.

The northwest Ohio oil and natural gas booms provided cheap fuel for factories. By the turn of the century Toledo was a supply and demand axis with major refineries and involvement in the newly emerging automobile industry. The Willys-Overland automobile company produced Jeeps during World War II,

becoming the nation's second largest auto company by the 1950's. Auto accessories and parts were a major industry as well. Toledo has been at the forefront of the labor movement and its strife. The Auto-Lite Strike in 1934 was a turning point. Two were killed when 1,600 workers clashed with the National Guard over union demands. A month later the union was in place. When much of the auto industry went overseas in the late Twentieth Century, Lucas County lost thousands of jobs, leading to an economic slump. The area got back to work to bring work back. Industry revived in the 1990's, cresting when Daimler Chrysler, ultimate successor to Willys, revived the Jeep plant in 1998 to build SUVs (sports utility vehicles).

For a community built on the backs of strong men, Lucas has encouraged opportunities for women. Suffragette Pauline Steinem and her granddaughter Gloria Steinem have led the way for women's rights. The first Girl Scout Troop, first YWCA, and first chapter of the Society for Professional and Business Women claim Toledo as home.

Lucas County took its name from Ohio's 12th Governor, Robert Lucas (1832-36).

LUCAS
TOLEDO SKYLINE

Toledo provides a wonderful, intimate urban environment. With this painting I found interest in the combination of old and new architecture and how well it is integrated within the city environment. It is very charming when seen from the riverwalk.

–Richard Otten

Toledo Skyline   20" x 20"   Oil on Canvas - Richard Otten

Madison

2000 Population - 40,213
Land Area - 465 Sq. Mi.
Persons/Sq. Mi. - 86.4

The vast expanse of fields one sees today in Madison County is a typical Ohio landscape. However, when the Native Americans inhabited the region and when the first white settlers arrived, it was an anomaly. Ninety-five percent of Ohio was covered with forests. The Darby Plains in Madison were an odd remnant from prehistoric times and considered unfit for anything but game hunting and fishing. Pioneers called it "The Barrens." The view was one of six-foot high grass stretching to the horizon with soil that was too wet to plow or plant. This Prairie Peninsula formed about 4,000 years ago when a drought period allowed the western prairie to grow where it was too dry for forest. By 1810, drainage and iron plow blades allowed cultivation. The fertile soil was uncovered and the prairie all but disappeared. Remnants of it exist in a few unplowed and ungrazed pockets along roadbeds and in cemeteries. Two examples of original prairie in Madison are the Bigelow and Smith Cemetery State Nature Preserves.

The first white settler in Madison County was Jonathan Alder in 1806. He was captured in Virginia as a boy and raised by Mingo Indians, often acting as a translator. He returned to Virginia to reunite with his mother and brought her and a new bride, Mary, back to settle. The log cabin Alder built along the Big Darby is now preserved in London, near Foster Cemetery where he is buried. Alder considered the Indians friends and mediated many issues between the remaining Native Americans and the new settlers. Madison became a county in 1810 with London as its seat.

The National Road (now U. S. Route 40) came through Madison County 1836-7. This highway not only allowed farmers to send their goods to other markets, it also gave access to London for the weekly livestock auctions. And come they did. Up to 3,000 people would crowd Courthouse Square to bid for the cattle shipped in from as far as Chicago and Cleveland. Good cattle here commanded the highest prices in the Midwest. When the railroads arrived in the 1850's, the stockyards were full as well. London has been the "Queen of Cattledom" since 1856. Still over ninety percent farmland, Madison produces fodder, ranking second in the state in soybeans and third in corn.

The National Road brought urban commerce to the otherwise rural county. Inns and taverns accommodated the lively travelers all along the National Road. One of the famed stopping places is the 1837 Red Brick Tavern in West Lafayette. Presidents Martin Van Buren and William Henry Harrison met here during their 1840 election contest. The guest list reads like a "Who's Who" of American history: John Quincy Adams, John Tyler, Andrew Jackson, Henry Clay and Daniel Webster, Horace Greeley, and Jenny Lind to name some of the more illustrious.

Madison County takes its name from James Madison, President when the county formed.

MADISON
THE RED BRICK TAVERN

This historic building has been a landmark for many people in this, my home county. I took some liberties with the actual scene which I sketched on site in February and replaced the trees which once were there, and changed it to a summer scene. I enjoyed trying to capture the light and shadows on the surface of the handmade russet brick walls.

—Mark Gingerich

The Red Brick Tavern   20" x 24"   Oil on Canvas - Mark Gingerich

Mahoning

2000 Population - 257,555
Land Area - 415 Sq. Mi.
Persons/Sq. Mi. - 620.2

The iron and steel industries have defined Mahoning County since Ohio's first charcoal iron furnace began producing in 1803 at Yellow Creek. David Tod, later governor of Ohio (1862-64), operated the area's first coal-fired blast furnace at Briar Hill in 1846. In the early years of the industry Mahoning competed with southern Ohio counties to supply iron to much of the young nation. When resources began failing in the latter area, northeastern Ohio took the state lead and held it until the 1950's. Steel succeeded iron. The Ohio Steel Company operated the first Bessemer steel mill in Mahoning beginning in 1895. Growing industries attracted immigrants to the mines and mills and the county grew accordingly. When Ohio chartered Mahoning in 1846, the county seat was Canfield. The locale moved to Youngstown in 1874.

Originally part of the Western Reserve, Mahoning holds the distinction of being the first area officially surveyed largely because the first surveyors sent to establish boundaries were able to find the line marking the nearby Pennsylvania border (stone posts with the letter P carved on top) as a starting point to plat the designated townships. In 1796, the southeast corner of the Reserve became Town One, Range One in what is now Poland Township. Towns such as Struthers and Lowellville thrived in the Nineteenth Century due to coal mining, which peaked in Mahoning County in the 1870's.

John Young, Youngstown's founder, profited from selling off his large Western Reserve landholdings. As a civic leader he wisely made some conditional sales such as the one to Isaac Powers and Phineas Hill to build a saw/gristmill on Mill Creek. It operated as a mill under various owners until 1888. Now restored from other uses, the mill reopened in 1985 in Mill Creek Metroparks.

As the steel industry and its auxiliary businesses grew in Mahoning, so did the problems, especially in Youngstown. Management/labor friction erupted numerous times in strikes and work stoppages as unions and federal regulations shaped national industry. Mahoning's legacy is the landmark legal decision of 1952, *The Youngstown Sheet and Tube vs. Sawyer* (President Truman's Secretary of Commerce). Truman had seized the steel mills during the Korean War, fearing a walkout when production was most needed to fight the war. The Supreme Court ultimately ruled the move unconstitutional putting the strongest ties on Presidential power until Watergate. Although the mill owners won that battle, they could not win other economic struggles, and Youngstown Sheet and Tube led the area decline until it closed the Campbell Works in 1977. U. S. Steel followed in 1979; Republic Steel, by 1982. Youngstown lost one-third of its population from 1960-80. Economic recovery has been slow, but there are on-going signs of progress.

Youngstown University has taken a leadership role in rebuilding by contributing workforce retraining and culture to the local economy. The Butler Institute of American Art, founded in 1919, has also remained a beacon of culture as America's first museum devoted to American art.

Mahoning takes its name from an Indian word meaning "at the lick."

MAHONING THE OLD MILL

The Beecher Foundations' restoration saved it! Lantermans' Mill was in pretty bad shape, last I saw it, but oh, what memories. Hikes down through the park on saturdays with Dad, playing in the creek below the falls. And to think, I actually didn't want to paint the mill originally. Was there really a need for another representation of it? Well, I'm certainly glad I did. The day was crisp and clear, the light was soft but bright, and I climbed down to a position along the creek that gave me a view that wasn't too frequently seen.

–Richard Canfield

The Old Mill   18" x 24"   Oil on Canvas - Richard Canfield

Marion

2000 Population - 66,217
Land Area - 404 Sq. Mi.
Persons/Sq. Mi. - 164.0

Marion steam shovels built the Panama Canal. They also built the Hoover and Boulder Dams and numerous other construction projects that shaped America. Marion Power Shovel was an industrial leader until closing in 1997.

Surveyor Jacob Foos located in the area in 1811 near a large underground natural spring. The settlement was called Jacob's Well before becoming Marion City. In mid-nineteenth century, Marion County and its seat Marion City were a major commercial hub in Ohio. The first road, now State Route 423, followed the Scioto Trail from Fremont to the Greenville Treaty line. The Indian path had been used by Harrison to transport supplies in the War of 1812. By the 1830's the canal system gave the area access to Cleveland and Columbus for farm products, especially corn and hogs. The railroads arrived in 1852 opening markets on a national scale and making Marion a huge rail center. County growth gained additional steam, literally, from the inventions of the revolving hay rake in 1863, and the steam shovel in 1874.

Marion bills itself as the "Popcorn Capital of the World" having both a Popcorn Festival and a Popcorn Museum. As well as its own product, Wyandot Foods produces popcorn for the Paul Newman brand and others. Where does popcorn taste its best? At the movies, of course. Integral to reviving Marion's downtown is the historic Palace Theatre. One of the twelve remaining out of the two hundred built by renowned theater architect John Eberson, the Palace was restored to its ornate glory in 1976.

Outside Marion, most of the county remains farmland. Of the seven villages in the county, tiny LaRue claims fame because it had the smallest National Football League team. The Oorang Indians played in the 1920's with Jim Thorpe as coach and player in 1922-3.

Much of the northern part of the county was virgin prairie. Several spots have survived farming and are preserves. The OSU Marion Prairie became a national landmark in 1988. One can also easily visit a sector along Route 98 untouched during railroad and road construction. The small Claridon Prairie has over seventy-five species of prairie flora.

The pride of Marion County is native son Warren G. Harding (1865-1923). Raised in the county, Harding moved to Marion City in 1884 to work for the *Marion Star*, where he rose to become its publisher. A well-liked, amiable man, Harding began his political career in the Ohio Senate, followed by Lieutenant Governor and U.S. Senator from Ohio. In a closely fought Republican Presidential nomination in 1920, Harding won on the tenth vote to run against fellow Ohioan James Cox. He waged his famous "front porch" campaign from his home in Marion, which is now the Harding Museum. Harding won handily and became the eighth U. S. President from Ohio. When Harding died of a stroke during a cross-county trip, the scandals of his presidency were just becoming known. Historians now assert that he was a trusting and naive man, many of whose appointees were corrupt. His hometown has honored Harding and his wife with a stately marble memorial and the museum.

Marion County was named for General Francis Marion, the Revolutionary War guerilla fighter who gained fame as "The Swamp Fox."

MARION
THE WAY IT WAS - CLARIDON PRARIE

The Claridon Prairie is a quiet sanctuary for nature and one of the last holdouts of the way things were originally. The locals hold bragging rights over this land they claim as truly indigenous, just ask Kensel Clutter. The view at the end of the prairie created an image that contrasted its peacefulness with almost geometric lines and angles. Despite that, it feels like my one "true" landscape.

–Richard Canfield

The Way it Was 20" x 30" Oil on Canvas - Richard Canfield

Medina

2000 Population - 151,095
Land Area - 424 Sq. Mi.
Persons/Sq. Mi. - 358.4

New Englanders settled Medina County and City. Joseph Harris founded the first town Harrisville, now Lodi, in 1811. The County was official soon after (1812) with Medina City as county seat. Founder Elijah Borden named the town Mecca but changed it upon realizing another Mecca already existed in Ohio. New England influence shows today in the layout of Medina City, with its town square and traditional New England architecture. A combination of Yankee ingenuity and pioneer quirkiness has hallmarked Medina's steady growth for two hundred years.

Many villages have interesting tales to tell. Settlers described a hellish swamp area as that "infernal region" and later named their town River Styx. Ironically, the town had the first business to experiment with sulfur matches.

Seville has a monument to the "Seville Giants," Captain Martin Vanuren Bates and his wife Anna, who retired there in 1873, after touring with the Barnum circus. Both the Bates were close to eight feet tall and weighed over 400 pounds. They had two children who weighed eighteen and twenty-three pounds. The latter died a few hours after birth, but is still the largest human newborn on record.

Hinckley remained a wilderness longer than much of the county because its Massachusetts owner, Judge Hinckley, held out on selling land until he could command a high price. As a result, many of the wild animals retreating from the settlements hid in the Judge's "preserve." On Christmas Day, 1818, neighbors from surrounding areas arranged a hunt to protect their livestock and killed hundreds of wild animals en masse. Storytellers credit the carcasses left after the hunt with attracting the turkey buzzards that have returned yearly ever since. Another explanation of the annual buzzard return comes from the 1808 hanging of a Wyandot woman accused of witchcraft. Her body was left to the scavengers. Whatever the true story, the buzzards do return every year to their summer home at Whipp's Ledges near Hinckley. Buzzard Day is celebrated March 15.

Ames Ives Root was a jeweler with eclectic interests. In 1865, he found an interest that would change his life and forge a family business – bees. Root had hundreds of hives and a new business within a few short years. He researched and wrote about bees including *The ABC's of Bee Culture*. His discoveries made honey a viable commercial product, especially when he invented a way to collect the honey without ruining the comb. The A. I. Root Company sent aviary supplies around the world. Called the "Honey King of America," Root ensured his place in Ohio history – Ohio has the majority of United States beekeepers, some 10,000 strong. His interest in cycling made him a familiar figure throughout northeast Ohio riding his velocipede, forerunner to the bicycle, and later models. Becoming friends with Dayton brothers who shared his interest, Root was present when the Wrights flew their craft on September 20, 1904. He wrote an article about the phenomena, but publishers scoffed at it as bizarre.

Medina is named for the city in Arabia to which Mohammed fled from Mecca.

View of Medina 20" x 30" Oil on Canvas - Tom Harbrecht

Meigs

2000 Population - 23,072
Land Area - 429 Sq. Mi.
Persons/Sq. Mi. - 53.7

Two remarkable earth products have sustained Meigs County growth from its 1819 official beginning — coal and salt. Valentine B. Horton funded drilling of the first salt well near Pomeroy. At its peak there were eighteen salt furnaces producing 3,600 barrels a day from Meigs. Horton also encouraged the coal industry in the early 1800's especially around Middleport, Minersville, and Syracuse. Today, American Electric Power Company runs a coal conveyer belt from South Central Coal in the west of the county to their Gavin generating plant fifteen miles away. The first county seat was Chester where Ohio's oldest standing courthouse now serves as the Appalachian Heritage Center.

Another natural resource, wood, also played an integral role in Meigs County. Reedsville and Belleville were boat-building centers. V. B. Horton built the world's first towboat in 1836 to transport his coal and salt. Captain Horatio Crooks introduced the compound cylinder steam engine. Middleport, so named because it is halfway between Pittsburgh and Cincinnati, was a favorite winter harbor for riverboats. One Samuel Clemons, aka Mark Twain, spent considerable time there visiting Captain Major John B. Downing who taught him the river boat trade. Twain wrote about Downing in his short story, "Alligator Jack." Twain's contemporary, writer Ambrose Bierce, hailed from Racine. During a career as peripatetic as Twain's, Bierce was a soldier, journalist, gold miner, and biting social commentator. Gregory Peck portrayed his life in the movie, *"Old Gringo."*

Pomeroy, the county seat, has been featured in *"Ripley's Believe it or Not"* twice. Built into the hills, Pomeroy has no cross streets because Main Street is along the riverfront. Secondly, the unique county courthouse is built into a hill so all three floors have ground level entrances. The county is frequently flooded, but came back strong from the devastating floods of 1834, 1913, and 1937.

Meigs County was the site of the only Civil War battle fought on Ohio soil. The Battle of Buffington Island (not an island) near Portland pitted Union Army forces under General Henry M. Judah against Morgan's Raiders. Future presidents Rutherford B. Hayes and William McKinley both fought in the battle. The Union Army routed Morgan's troops and led to his ultimate capture. Daniel McCook, patriarch of the fighting McCooks, was mortally injured; a monument to him is at Buffington Island Park.

Pomeroy's J. Edwin Campbell (1867-95) was a teacher in Rutland before becoming an author and the first president of West Virginia Colored Institute, later West Virginia State University. His published works include *Driftings and Gleanings*. The Reverend John Joseph Jessing served at Sacred Heart Church, Pomeroy, as his first parish. While there he started an orphan asylum and a German newspaper to support it. In 1888, he started the Collegium Josephinum in Columbus to train priests to minister to the Germans. The Josephinum received pontifical status in 1892; it is the only seminary outside Italy overseen by the Vatican.

The earth itself provides the most recent economic impetus to Meigs. The rich floodplain soil produces truck farming vegetables and a burgeoning floriculture business; greenhouses are also opening. Herbs are big business, too, with the Center for the Preservation of Medicinal Herbs headquartered in Rutland.

Meigs County was named for Return Jonathan Meigs, Jr., Ohio Governor and U. S. Postmaster General.

MEIGS
RIVERTOWN, POMEROY

This view looks down Court Street to the Ohio River, (West Virginia in the distance). I'm standing on the balcony of the Meigs County Court House. Both my parents were born and raised in Pomeroy. Before they were married, my Dad lived one block from here and my Mom a couple of miles up river in Minersville. As a kid, I spent man hours in this town.

–Tom Harbrecht

Rivertown, Pomeroy, Ohio   16" x 20"   Oil on Canvas - Tom Harbrecht

Mercer

2000 Population - 23,072
Land Area - 463 Sq. Mi.
Persons/Sq. Mi. - 88.3

The skyline rising above this very flat region tells a visible story of Mercer County. From several vantage points one can see many spires of the "Land of Cross-tipped Churches" and just as many silver-topped grain silos. Farming and religion have shaped Mercer County's culture since its largely German settlers began arriving in the 1830's.

Before the pioneers could safely settle, hundreds of Governor St. Clair's men died in attempts to subdue Native Americans. General "Mad" Anthony Wayne built Fort Recovery on the site of the 1791 surprise attack by Little Turtle's warriors on St. Clair's troops where over 600 soldiers had perished. A reconstructed version of the fort is open for visitors today. An 1817 treaty officially cleared the Indians from the area. The county was chartered in 1820 with Celina as its county seat.

Initially, the area thrived from the lumber mills as the immigrants turned the forests into farmland. The Miami Canal opened venues for farm products which have sustained the local economy ever since. Mercer is now first in the State in swine, second in corn production, and third in cattle and milk cows.

Grand Lake Saint Mary's State Park, originally Grand Reservoir, was an important part of the canal system. The lake was built between 1837-45 as a feeder to stabilize canal water depth. Workers labored to dig by hand both the lake and the three-mile feeder to the canal. They were paid thirty-five cents per day and a jigger of whiskey to ward off malaria. This incredible feat created the world's largest artificial lake at that time. The lake has been a major natural resource and recreational facility since the canal era ended. During the 1890's oil boom, dozens of oil derricks dotted the lake. A pile of rocks in the middle marks the location of the last producing well in the lake. Ohio made Grand Lake Saint Mary's its first State Park in 1949. The lake lies on one of the nation's major bird migration routes. Varieties of ducks, geese, heron, swans, and egrets are among the millions of birds flying and resting here spring and fall.

The lake project brought settlers and drained swampy land so that farming could thrive. The settlers, of course, brought much of their ways of life with them. Faith was integral to those cultures. Mostly German Catholic but from various regions of "the old country," each small congregation worked to build a church styled like the one they had left behind. Now, some two dozen churches dot scenic routes, especially in the southern part of the county, and draw visitors for services and sightseeing. The tallest building in the county is the tower of St. Charles Seminary, now a home for retired priests and brothers of the Missionaries of the Precious Blood.

Augustus Wattles was a Quaker with a vision. He led freed slaves to Mercer County and helped them establish the town of Carthagena.

Mercer County was named in honor of General Hugh Mercer, a Revolutionary War hero. He died in the Battle of Princeton in 1777.

MERCER
CELINA AS VIEWED ACROSS LAKE
ST. MARYS

I chose to paint Mercer County on a tranquil fall day from Windy Point on the southern shore of Lake St. Marys. I found this lovely spot on the bank of the lake where a clump of trees was silhouetted nicely against the sky and lake, while taking in a view of the city of Celina in the distance.

–Mark Gingerich

Celina as Viewed Across Lake St. Marys   24" x 20"   Oil on Canvas - Mark Gingerich

Miami

2000 Population - 98,868
Land Area - 407 Sq. Mi.
Persons/Sq. Mi. - 242.9

History is often about heroes and battles, but unsung heroes and averted battles can make just as strong an impact on our world. Miami County has both. Being on the Ohio frontier, the area had its share of conflict. After Miami Chief Memeska allowed the British to establish a trade center, Fort Pickawillany, deep in French territory, the French retaliated with a band of raiders who attacked and burned the post. They took their British captives to Detroit for execution. This early incident in the French and Indian Wars was a prelude to decades of strife. Fort Piqua, built in 1793, was a supply post for General William Henry Harrison's western trek. General "Mad" Anthony Wayne erected log breastworks at Covington that he named Fort Rowdy because of his soldiers' behavior as they wintered there. Miami County was safe for settlement and became a county in 1807. When the original county seat of Staunton did not thrive nor have a courthouse, leaders created a new town for that purpose, Troy. The 1888 courthouse with its five iron domes, was designed by Ohioan J. W. Yost.

The country owes John Johnston, a quiet hero, gratitude for that peaceful settlement. He was Indian Agent for Western Ohio from 1812-29, negotiating several treaties and the takeover of many Indian lands. The Wyandots, among the last to leave, praised him to President Monroe in 1819. Johnston's farm is now part of the Piqua Historical Area. It abuts Canal Lock #8 and a remnant of the canal. Johnston was also state canal commissioner. The Ohio-Erie came through Miami in 1837.

Troy was an integral part of the Underground Railroad with many unrecorded citizens helping move fleeing slaves along to freedom. Unsung hero John Randolph from Virginia contributed to Miami County lives by freeing his slaves and settling them at Rossville, just outside Piqua. Pennsylvania Quakers migrated to West Milton and built a meetinghouse in 1804. Today it is the Union Township Historical Museum and Quaker Research Center. This group raised Quaker eyebrows when they built a church with a steeple reaching toward heaven, against their prevailing culture.

Contributors to aviation from Miami County also deserve recognition. Dominick S. Gentile was a World War I flying ace. The Weaver Aircraft Company, WACO, was the center of the civilian aircraft industry. They built six hundred UPF planes for the civilian training program prior to World War II. Nancy Decker Sherlock, an astronaut onboard the Discovery, also hails from Miami.

County native A. B. Graham is a hero to thousands of farm youth and their families because he started the boys and girls clubs that later became Four-H Clubs. While evidence of his influence is in projects all over the county, a Memorial Center honors him in Conover.

Other Miami County celebrities include the Mills Brothers from Piqua. The group's songs such as "Glowworm" and "Paper Doll" are beloved American standards.

Miami County took its name for the Miami Indians, who lived there until the 1750's.

Miami
LOCK #8

The Johnston Farm worked in the Piqua Historical Area let us see Lock #8 of the Erie-Miami Canal, which is a historical working lock. We drove through the beautiful and closed historic farm acreage and literally took a trip back in time to reach the Lock. I painted a head-on view through the lock's opening and the canal itself is utterly exquisite. This was early evening and overcast weather, but our good fortune made us happy plein air pioneers!

–Kaye Michele Darling

Lock #8   24" x 36"   Oil on Canvas - Kaye Michele Darling

Monroe

2000 Population - 15,180
Land Area - 456 Sq. Mi.
Persons/Sq. Mi. - 33.3

Hills have seemed impediments to settlement to some and inducements to others. Europeans came to the county expressly because the hills on the Ohio River reminded them of their native land. Although the first white settlers arrived in Jackson Township in the 1790's, riverside trappers' hamlets were already doing business. In 1814, Archibald Woods established Woodsfield. The first building there was Spencer Biddle's tavern. Monroe County was chartered in 1813 with Woodsfield as its county seat.

A Swiss contingent going down the Ohio on a raft in 1819 were attracted to the rugged landscape and decided to stay. When one of those who greeted them could speak German, the flatboat group was convinced to settle on government land and "Ohio's Switzerland" was born. The thin county soil was difficult to farm, but the Swiss turned their land into profitable dairy ventures. Cheese, especially Swiss and Limburger, became an important export.

Towns on the river thrived with river business. Fly got its moniker because it was easy to pronounce and remember. Residents deny the name came from the noxious garbage-eating insect. The sternwheeler ferry between Fly and Sisterville, West Virginia, ran as early as 1804. A nearby bronze marker indicates where George Washington slept when he surveyed the area. Clarington, Hannibal, and Sardis were boat-building centers with famous riverboat men residing there. Sardis' first exports were castor beans and ginseng. The town pump sitting in the middle of Muskingum and Mound Streets since the early 1800's continues to be the water choice of some Sardis residents. Now housed in its own gazebo, the pump was electrified in 1952. Hannibal's modernization has included huge river locks built by the Army Corps of Engineers. Kiedaish Point, a 1,332' overlook near Hannibal, has a spectacular view of the Ohio River Valley.

The uphill interior of Monroe County developed later. Woodsfield grew slowly because of its inaccessibility. The first courthouse was wood, followed by brick. The current Greek-style building with a stained-glass dome was built in 1906. Dairy and cattle farms dominate the landscape. The first Monroe County Fair in 1850 awarded the top prizes of $5.00 each to the best wine and the best stallion. Prizes of $1.00 each were given to butter, cheese, and blanket makers. The Amish community at Calais runs several sawmills. Half of the county is part of the Wayne National Forest, re-establishing the vast timber growth. When railroads made passage into the mid-county easier, gristmill and timber products became important to the economy. The narrow gauge Bellaire, Zanesville, and Cincinnati Railroad, better known as the Bent, Zigzag, and Crooked, serviced the county until 1931. The Black Walnut Festival celebrates logging with lumberjack contests, skidding, knuckle booms, and old-fashioned crafts.

As a tiny footnote to the lumber business, the Matchstick Jack Memorial Museum in Sardis has over one hundred handcrafted items made from wooden matchsticks and toothpicks. The crafters use over 100,000 matches per year to make their wares.

Monroe County takes its name from James Monroe, Secretary of State at the time the county was formed. He later became the fifth U. S. President.

Monroe
NORTHERN VIEW FROM KIEDAISCH POINT

I was given this county to paint a week after I had finished my originally designated paintings. It was thrilling to be back on the road in Ohio. Monroe County is beautiful, full of hills, trees and lovely farms; but I found my heart looking out across the Ohio River. High at the top of Kiedaisch Point, one can look north or south, or east into West Virginia. It was quiet, except for the occasional sound of a train on the West Virginia side, or a barge going up river. I chose to paint the northern view because of the shapes; because I had already painted bridges; because I hadn't painted a factory. The factory wasn't the reason for the painting, it just happened to be there. The day was cloudy, the view was stunning, and the Ohio River "just kept rolling along."

–Debra Joyce Dawson

Northern View From Kiedaisch Point   20" x 16"   Oil on Canvas - Debra Joyce Dawson

Montgomery

2000 Population - 559,062
Land Area - 462 Sq. Mi.
Persons/Sq. Mi. - 1,210.9

2003 is not only the Bicentennial of Ohio' but also the Centennial of Wilbur and Orville Wright's invention of the first heavier-than-air practical flying machine. Events throughout the year drew visitors from around the world to celebrate that marvelous achievement in the Wrights' hometown, Dayton, culminating on December 17, the official anniversary of the first flight. What is really being celebrated, though, is the fruition of an idea, inventiveness made practical. Montgomery County has nourished hundreds of inventions; it holds more patents per capita than any other county in America.

The very earliest known inhabitants of the area, the Fort Ancient peoples, built an extraordinary village now being reconstructed as Sunwatch. Archeologists are discovering the scientific sophistication of these early Native Americans from the solar calendar at the center of the area and other artifacts. Historic Indians hunted and lived here before the various wars fought heavily in the area. The Greenville Treaty brought peace to the frontier making settlement safe. Dayton was organized in 1796, but that proved to be illegal, a situation that was remedied in 1805 when Daniel Cooper covered the debt to the U.S. Government and passed on legal titles to the settlers. Montgomery County was recognized in 1803, with Dayton as its seat.

Farming was the early economic backbone of the county, as it was throughout Ohio. The Shaker colony established at Watervliet in 1806 brought a group with uncommon ingenuity to the area. The village sustained itself by selling high-quality seed, produce, and stocking yarn. Watervliet's few remaining members moved to Union Village in 1900. Montgomery population and commerce exploded during the Civil War with the railroads and constant movement of troops through the area. Industry thrived from technical innovations of all sorts. John Patterson recognized the brilliance of the Ritty brothers who in 1879 contrived a way to mechanically keep track of their bar's sales and cash. Patterson eventually bought them out and established National Cash Register, NCR. In the process, Patterson's creativity emerged when he "invented" direct advertising by mailing daily product announcements to area merchants. Patterson also hired Charles Kettering who eventually held over 300 patents, especially for the automobile industry, most notably the electric starter. Thomas Watson quarreled with Patterson and left to found his own company – now IBM.

The Wrights rightly deserve credit for their invention and improvements, but others in Montgomery County also contributed to aeronautics with the first parachute, solo instrument flight, night flying advances, world altitude records, space food, and aerial photography. Wright-Patterson Air Force Base houses the U. S. Air Force Museum. The Wright Brothers' friend Paul Laurence Dunbar was one of America's first great African American authors.

The uncommon number of common innovations affects us all everyday from Dr. W. H. Church's inventing cellophane tape to John Morton's parking meters; from E. T. Fraze's pull tab and pop top cans to C. F. Jenkins' movie projector, camera, and film. Life-changing medical break throughs like L. Clark's heart-lung machine and ultra-scientific discoveries such as Janning's work with liquid crystals have enriched the world from Montgomery County, Ohio.

Montgomery County took its name from Revolutionary War hero General Richard Montgomery who died fighting at Quebec.

MONTGOMERY
THE WRIGHT'S SHOP

The unique element in this scene, painted one warm April afternoon on site, was in contemplating the significance of the building where a new era of human air travel in the world became a reality. I was painting in sporadic clouds of dust from the workers in front of the building who were paving the road with bricks.

–Mark Gingerich

The Wright's Shop 24" x 20" Oil on Canvas - Mark Gingerich

Morgan

2000 Population - 14,897
Land Area - 418 Sq. Mi.
Persons/Sq. Mi. - 35.7

In the early Twentieth Century James Ball Naylor's western genre novels were all the rage. His tales of Indians, pioneers, and frontier life excited readers' imaginations as they highlighted history in such works as *"In the Days of St. Clair"* and *"Mad Anthony's Banner."* Much of Naylor's material is based on the area in which he grew up and its lore. The foothills of Morgan County's Appalachia are serene and scenic now, but remnants of a rich and raucous past still dot the county.

The first attempt to settle Morgan County was thwarted by Delaware and Wyandot Indians. The Native Americans attacked a small group of whites encamped in an unfortified stockade at Big Bottom early in 1791. Twelve settlers died, two escaped and five became prisoners. Ohio has memorialized the incident that was the start of four years of frontier warfare.

Settlement resumed after the War of 1812. Robert McConnel created McConnelsville, which became the county seat the same year that Morgan became a county, 1817. Mills and foundries were the first industries followed quickly by salt. Morgan was Ohio's premier salt producer from 1820 to 1840. Coal was a major industry, especially strip mining around Bristol and Manchester townships. The last remaining mill on the Muskingum River is at Lock Number 7. The current structure at Stockport replaced several earlier mills in 1906. It provided hydroelectric power for the village and served as a feed mill until it closed in 1997. Now an inn, the Mill once again serves as a catalyst for county growth.

Frontier culture was a mixture of the crude and the civilized. Malta had a five by twelve foot dungeon next to the town hall for rioters, adulterers, and petty larcenists. A one-room schoolhouse has been moved to the adjoining site. This same town produced Naylor and his sister Leila Naylor Morris, a noted musician who wrote over 1,000 gospel songs. Tales about the coal-mining town of San Toy abound. There was a gunfight over a twenty-dollar debt that left one man dead and the other critically wounded, both lying in the street. Robbers took the coal company payroll and rode out of town on horseback just

like in the movies. Fires destroyed the mineshafts so that the nineteen remaining voters agreed to abandon the town in 1931.

McConnelsville exemplifies efforts toward civility with its 1858 Greek revival courthouse and one of the few Opera Houses left in the state. In continuous use since 1890, the Opera House was McConnelsville's first building to be lighted by electricity. Town favorite son, Howard Chandler Christy (1872-1952), was famous for his Spanish American War and World War I recruiting posters. In the 1920's, Christy painted his masterworks. "The Signing of the Constitution of the United States" hangs in the U. S. Capitol and "The Signing of the Greenville Treaty" is in the Ohio Statehouse.

Today, western Morgan County's State Route 78 between Glouster and McConnelsville is called "The Rim of the World" for its spectacular scenery along a hairpin-curved drive. The road is also listed as one of the best roads in the nation on which sports car drivers might test their skills.

Morgan County takes its name from Revolutionary War General David Morgan who defeated the British Army at Cowpens, South Carolina, in 1781.

MORGAN
STOCKPORT LOCKS

I didn't realize the Muskingum River dropped in elevation, and so I found the locks interesting. The Locks at Stockport sit next to a fairly modern bridge that takes you to Stockport. I included the Stockport Mill across the Muskingum River.

–Tom Harbrecht

Stockport Locks #6   16" x 26"   Oil on Canvas - Tom Harbrecht

Morrow

2000 Population - 31,628
Land Area - 406 Sq. Mi.
Persons/Sq. Mi. - 77.9

Morrow is one of the few areas in Ohio where no significant warfare has occurred. The remains of the prehistoric Moundbuilder Native American culture has yielded no war artifacts. Historic Native Americans such as the Delaware, Shawnee and Wyandot traveled through the county using it as a shared hunting ground until white settlement made game scarce. There are no recorded Indian villages. The numerous frontier battles during the Ohio's march to statehood went around Morrow County, leaving no known historic sites. Pioneers poured into north central Ohio shortly after the War of 1812. Most coming to Morrow County were from the eastern middle states. A significant number came from Wales. Most cleared land to farm. A sizable group of Quakers built Mt. Pleasant in 1815, among them Thomas Rotch (1767-1823), an early abolitionist activist.

The most legendary "fight" in Morrow County history occurred when it struggled to become a separate county from the surrounding ones, and included a "fight" over the county seat. The need to create a new county came from local citizens who wanted more accessible civil functions such as real estate transactions and other legal business. After much politicking between Whigs and Democrats, and among the affected counties who did not want to lose power and revenue, the 1847 Ohio legislature agreed to the petition to take parts of Delaware, Knox, Richland and Marion counties to form Morrow. One vote hinged on naming the county Morrow at the behest of a Warren County legislator. The concurrent fight to name a county seat is still a much-told story. Both Chesterville and Mt.Gilead emerged as frontrunners to have the "capital" honor. Several Mt.Gilead supporters were able to get a known card player who favored Chesterville into a game that lasted so long it kept him from addressing the voting session. Legend also says the room was locked from the outside in case the game ended prematurely. Mt Gilead won the vote and the Ohio legislature charted Morrow County in 1848.

Railroads came through in the 1830's and 1840's, making bustling railroad villages of Marengo and West Gilead, which later changed its name to Edison.

Farmers were able then to expand their product markets. Still one of the state's most rural counties with over sixty percent of the land in farming, Morrow today is a leading sheep center. Small businesses have accompanied agriculture, however. One early prominent businessman, Dr. Nathan Tucker, sold his famed "Asthma Specific" patent medicine from Mr. Gilead and drew people from all over the state. While his business did not last, transportation on modern highways has again made Morrow County accessible for small businesses in a central location.

One of the two town squares in Mt. Gilead honors a more united effort of Morrow County. The obelisk in the North Square memorializes citizens who gave their wealth during World War I. Morrow County had the highest per capita Liberty Bond sales of any Ohio county. A grateful government erected the monument as a "thank you" for that effort.

Morrow County is the namesake of Jeremiah Morrow. He was an Ohio Congressman, U. S. Senator, and Ohio's Governor from 1822-1826.

MORROW
VICTORY SHAFT, MT. GILEAD

I liked this World War I memorial obelisk in Mt. Gilead. This intersection functions much like a European round-a-bout. The tidy landscaped memorial is also protected at all four corners by "sentry-like" traffic lights. I chose a simple view of the monument.

–Tom Harbrecht

Victory Shaft, Mt. Gilead, Ohio   26" x 28"   Oil on Canvas - Tom Harbrecht

Muskingum

2000 Population - 84,585
Land Area - 665 Sq. Mi.
Persons/Sq. Mi. - 127.3

Muskingum County has thrived due to its natural resources from flint and salt to water and clay soil, but it is the creativity of its people and how they have utilized those resources that make this county unique. Both the prehistoric and later Woodland Native Americans sought the flint from Flint Ridge that runs through here and adjoining counties. Likewise, the nearby salt licks were valuable not only for the salt itself, but because it drew animals for good hunting. Zane's Trace, Ohio's first road, followed Indian trails. Ebenezer Zane was rewarded for laying the road with acreage at each intersection of a river. The land that intersected with the Muskingum River Zane gave to his son-in-law John McIntire, who named the 1797 settlement Zanesville. Muskingum County was chartered in 1803 with Zanesville as the county seat.

Increase Mathews bought land from Marietta's Rufus Putnam across the river from Zanesville and started a rival town, Putnam. Creative town residents hoped to win the state capital contest so they built a potential capitol building in 1809. When Columbus won out, the building reverted to a meeting place and school; now it is a museum. During the Civil War Zanesville supported slavery, while Putnam was abolitionist and an Underground Railroad stop. The Presbyterian Church was center of anti-slavery activity; William Beecher, brother of Harriet Beecher, was its first pastor. Zanesville finally absorbed Putnam in the 1870's.

Clay from the rolling hills helped Zanesville be the heart of the pottery industry. While much of the industry has closed or moved operations abroad, a revival is drawing connoisseurs to the county for collectibles, shows, and the eight remaining producing potteries. McCoy, once the largest U.S. manufacturer, and Robinson-Ransbottom in Roseville, now one of the world's largest stoneware producers, are huge operations, along with several smaller specialty businesses. Additionally, there are several pottery museums in the county and the Ohio Ceramic Center between Roseville and Crooksville.

Unusual architecture has roots in Muskingum as well. Zanesville's Y-bridge is the fifth on its site since 1814. Moses Dillon helped design the five "S" bridges on the National Road. County native architect Cass Gilbert (1859-1934) designed the Minnesota, Arkansas, and West Virginia state capitols, the U. S. Supreme Court Building, and the Woolworth Building, at the time the world's tallest.

County recognition has come as much from literature as history. Zane Gray (1875-1939), grandson of Ebenezer, was the nation's most popular author in the first half of the 20th Century. *Riders of the Purple Sage* and his many other western novels have readers worldwide. Writer/translator/singer Jean Starr Untermeyer (1886-1970) used the German culture from Zanesville to translate German poetry and in the 1920's become a singer in Germany. She and her husband, critic and editor Louis Untermeyer, held a New York salon for literary luminaries such as Frost, Millay, Sandburg, and Pound.

Astronaut and Senator John Glenn is New Concord's native son. His recently moved boyhood home there is now a museum. In 1962 Glenn was the first American to orbit the earth and was a U. S. Senator when he took his return voyage in 1998 to become the oldest person to travel in space.

Muskingum County takes it name from a Delaware Indian word meaning "town by a river."

MUSKINGUM
FOREST ON FLINT RIDGE

I painted from the home of a childhood friend who lives in Hopewell along the Flint Ridge in Muskingum County. After a day of searching through shards of flint and earthy finds, it was fun being in Flint Ridge's surrounding forest before making our way back to the city noise. This old forest brings about many conversations to family friends who come to find ancient relics.

–*Kaye Michele Darling*

Forest on Flint Ridge   30" x 24"   Oil on Canvas - Kaye Michele Darling

Noble

2000 Population - 14,058
Land Area - 399 Sq. Mi.
Persons/Sq. Mi. - 35.2

The youngest claims the oldest and a great deal of history in between. Noble County is the last-formed of the eighty-eight Ohio counties. In a political move to create another Whig seat in Ohio, Noble was formed from parts of the surrounding counties in 1851. The act did not achieve that goal, but did create a county seat, Sarahsville, nearer to the remote population of the area. The seat moved to Caldwell village when it began in a more central location in 1857. The Noble County boundaries are so crooked that the county line has thirty corners.

One of the earliest settlers in the county was John Gray in 1803. He had worked for George Washington at Mount Vernon after mustering out of the Revolutionary War army. Gray had seen action at Williamsburg and was present at Yorktown when the British surrendered. When he died in 1868 at 104 years of age, Gray was the last surviving pensioner from the Revolution. His tombstone reads, "The Last of Washington's Companions."

The first white settlers were farmers and mill operators. Johnny Appleseed, nee Chapman, visited the area frequently enough that people from all over sent hundreds of rocks and pebbles from places Johnny had planted trees to erect a monument to him near Dexter City. He had relatives buried nearby. The county's Allegheny Plateau ridges and hills are considered to be the best apple-growing district in the state. Applejack and corn squeezin's were early popular Noble products along with tobacco and wool.

While at first considered to be a nuisance in salt production, the first oil well in the United States gushed in Noble County in 1814. Robert McKee was looking for salt brine and initially the oil was considered good only for medicinal purposes as a tonic. "Seneca Oil" was bottled and sold for whatever ailed ya.' When oil refining became a reality, the oil boom sustained the county through the 1870's and 1880's. The original well still produces oil in small quantities.

Coal mining ebbed and waned in Noble, too. Belleville, for example, went overnight from being a tiny whistle stop to a coal town that peaked in 1920 with a population of 1,000 people and fourteen saloons. Rumors declared the town to be a great one for fist fighting. Indicative of rough-and-tumble coal miners and inflation, the town of Matrim was renamed Soakum because of the high prices charged to travelers for liquor. The locale now encourages visitors with the Soakum Festival of old-time activities such as apple-butter-making and crafts. Little coal is produced in Noble now, but the Miner's Memorial Park features a huge reminder of those days. The Big Muskie power shovel was one of the seven engineering wonders of the world when it was used for strip mining. The drag bucket rests in the park for tourist wonderment. The bucket weighs 460,000 pounds and is the size of a twelve-car garage!

The rural area was witness to history in 1925, when the Navy dirigible Shenandoah crashed in a storm near Ava (immediately east of today's Interstate 77) during a tour to state fairs. The airship broke in two, killing fourteen of those aboard including Captain Lansdowne, the top expert in lighter-than-air transports. There were nineteen survivors. This and the Hindenburg disaster spelled the end of the era for rigid air ships.

Noble County is named for pioneer James Noble who first bought land here in 1814.

NOBLE
ON THE FARM

Growing up in Ohio, I developed an affinity for the architecture of farms. I have always liked the sounds, sights and moods that farms provide. I painted this scene because it reminds me of so many farms in Ohio. I wanted to include this idea in how I see Ohio.

–Richard Otten

On the Farm   24" x 36"   Oil on Canvas - Richard Canfield

Ottawa

2000 Population - 40,985
Land Area - 255 Sq. Mi.
Persons/Sq. Mi. - 160.8

Ottawa County is all about water. Ottawa's mainland sliver was wrested from marsh and swampland. The Portage River provides transportation. Even the inland cities recall water – Genoa and Oak Harbor. Thirteen glacier-formed islands make up the rest of the county.

Glacial activity made Lake Erie the shallowest of the Great Lakes, giving it a habitat conducive to more varieties and numbers of fish than any of the others Great Lakes. Fish include yellow perch, white bass, small mouth bass, and Erie's signature fish, walleye. Native Americans came through the area establishing small settlements on some of the islands and on the mainland. Oliver Hazard Perry ensured American ownership by his victory over the British fleet in waters of Ottawa County in 1813. When Perry inspired his out-manned and out-gunned navy by jumping from his sinking Lawrence to the Niagara and hoisting his personal "Don't Give up the Ship" flag, the troops rallied and overcame the British. Perry's message to his superiors was, "We have met the enemy and they are ours." The world's tallest Doric column, Perry's Victory and International Peace Memorial in Put-in-Bay, commemorates the event.

Settlement was slow, but constant. Port Clinton, the first village, was literally settled by accident. Stranded shipwreck survivors built a town at the mouth of the Portage River. The fishing supported early settlers, followed by limestone quarrying and gypsum mining. Oak Harbor and Genoa (1835) grew from the timber business, shipped upriver and out from Port Clinton. When the canals passed the area by, Ottawa residents built the second railroad in Ohio, the Mad River Railroad. After the timber was gone, the fertile soil and latest-freezing weather in Ohio were ideal for fruit and vegetable farming, which continues. Genoa also boasts a unique attraction, Our House, the only "outhouse" on the National Historic Register. Not an ordinary structure, this one is Romanesque Revival complete with arches. The facility is an eight-seater with separate entrances for men and women, boys and girls.

Marblehead stone quarries still produce limestone. The Marblehead lighthouse, the longest continuously operating light in the Great Lakes, guards the peninsula. The lighthouse park also includes the lighthouse keeper's cottage. The state's first woman keeper, Rachel Wolcott, took over the care in 1832 when her husband died.

Lakeside Village originated as a Methodist campground in the 1870's. The leaders applied the Chautauqua concept to the religious camp meetings. Tents gradually gave way to a hotel and quaint houses, many of which are still owned by the original families. Lakeside still thrives with special programming each summer.

Each island has it own special history of everything from playground for the rich to wildlife refuge. Civil War financier Jay Cooke built a mansion on Gibraltar for occasional entertaining of Presidents and industry barons before his family gave it to The Ohio State University for research. Rutherford B. Hayes owned Mouse Island as a summer home. South Bass is the largest and the most popular for visitors; the Strontium Crystal Cave at Heineman's winery is one of the two largest known geodes on the planet. Middle Bass is famed for the now-defunct Lonz Winery and Ohio's newest state park.

Ottawa County is named for the Indian tribe. The name means "trader."

OTTAWA
THE MARBLEHEAD LIGHT

I sketched around the Marblehead Lighthouse on a cool breezy spring day. The sun was breaking out and retreating constantly, making it difficult to focus on the light effect. I selected a spot just off the rocky beach with sun breaking through the hazy afternoon sky behind the lighthouse.

–Mark Gingerich

The Marblehead Light   24" x 18"   Oil on Canvas - Mark Gingerich

Paulding

2000 Population - 20,293
Land Area - 416 Sq. Mi.
Persons/Sq. Mi. - 48.8

The Great Black Swamp covered what is now Paulding County with dense forests and knee-deep muck. To take the territory away from the British and their Native American allies, General William Henry Harrison built a string of Forts along the Maumee and Auglaize Rivers. His troops used Fort Brown on the banks of the Auglaize as a supply depot from 1812-15. After the War, the county was safe, but inhospitable. There were enough settlers along the Auglaize for Paulding to become official in 1820, but little settlement occurred until workers moved in to build the Wabash-Erie and the Miami-Erie Canals. The two met in Junction, which grew to rival Fort Wayne, Indiana, as a center of commerce.

Some hardy Irish and German immigrants bought land here because it was so cheap. They cleared the trees, but getting rid of the stumps and digging drainage ditches took years. A layer of clay just under the surface prevented natural drainage, and the land was so flat there was almost no natural runoff. Finally, in 1859, the Ohio legislature passed laws allowing public money for ditches, and settlement became rapid. The timber business was augmented by the tile business as numerous small kiln operations supplied the red clay tiles needed to line the ditches. Some of the best agricultural land in the state emerged from the swamp and Paulding has been agricultural ever since. More than eighty per cent of the county is farmland with grains and soybeans as the leading crops.

The Paulding County Courthouse in Paulding City was built in 1886 as a centennial memorial and symbol of the success of residents in taming the wilderness. Another source of pride is the first Carnegie library built for a county rather than a city. Andrew Carnegie promised a building if land was donated and he could approve design plans. Rebecca Latty donated four lots in town. The same Columbus firm that designed the Hayes Memorial in Fremont, Howard and Merriman, designed the new library, which opened in 1912.

Paulding honors its Great Black Swamp heritage with several natural resource places of interest. The Black Swamp Nature Center is a newly expanded park and outdoor education center located on a main bird migration route. The swamp still sustains an incredible diversity. At this park birders and students can enjoy three distinct habitats: woodland, marshland, and meadowland. The designated scenic part of the Maumee River runs from the Indiana border to the U.S. Route 24 bridge. The meandering flood plain drains a 5,000 - square mile watershed, and farmers are working on no-till and other ecologically viable farming methods to prevent and overcome pollution. Otto Ehrhart from the area compiled Ohio's largest nature collection by an individual with over 500 preserved birds, 7,000 insects, 1,200 bird eggs and numerous reptiles and mammals. Antwerp City Hall houses Ehrhart's natural history museum.

Paulding County takes its name from John Paulding who was one of the three soldiers to capture British spy Major John Andre in 1780.

PAULDING
GRAVES AT MOUNT ZION
BAPTIST CHURCH

We followed county roads hoping to find an aptly described "tiny white church" called The Zion Baptist Church. We found it quickly and a puppy and her mother came out to greet us as I quickly set up my easel with eagerness to block out a field painting of this little building with a big story nestled along the Little Auglaize River. The presence of the three lone graves in its churchyard were a reminder of times past and I was drawn to the sad equation of my father's war stories from World War II of black soldiers not being quartered with white soldiers, along with other exclusions. The long markers are of three such soldiers whose friends and family visit this church each year as reminders that must remain with history as we move forward as a nation.

–Kaye Michele Darling

Graves at Mt. Zion Baptist Church   16" x 20"   Oil on Canvas - Kaye Michele Darling

Perry

2000 Population - 34,078
Land Area - 410 Sq. Mi.
Persons/Sq. Mi. - 83.2

Ohio history is filled with great upheaval as booms in resources have given way to depletion and changed economics. So often timber, iron, salt, coal, water – the bases of Ohio's early growth – have been depleted or replaced with new technologies. Perry County is different. Newly discovered or long exploited resources continue to be produced; the industries they support survive. Coal and clay made the county, and still reign. Perry County is first in Ohio for production of coal and hematite iron ore. The vast strata of clay have kept the pottery business viable and world-renowned.

In the early 1800's German immigrants began settling towns such as Somerset and Thornville. Perry County dates officially to 1817, with Somerset as its county seat. That changed to New Lexington in 1857. The building of the National Road brought many Irish to the area, among them the Sheridan family. A statue of Civil War General Philip H. Sheridan astride his horse Rienzi stands in Somerset. Sheridan helped his father and the road building by driving mule wagons, but a mentor saw enough potential leadership in the small, feisty teen to secure him an appointment to West Point. In spite of a suspension for fighting, Sheridan graduated; he is best known for his charge through the Shenandoah Valley that led to Lee's surrender at Appomattox.

A New Lexington son, and different sort of fighter, was Januarius MacGahan. Told he was too young to be a teacher, he became a war correspondent in Europe. His tales of the Turkish horrors inflicted on the Balkans brought Russia into the cause. When MacGahan rode in with the troops, he was hailed as the "Liberator of Bulgaria." The Journalism Hall of Fame inducted MacGahan in 1928.

Ohio's first Catholic Church is St. Joseph's in Somerset, started in 1818. The Dominican complex had a convent, Friary, church, school, and college, many of which burned 1864. Most were rebuilt by 1880 and are still in use.

The pottery industry began in the 1820's with many small specialty operations. New Lexington produced terra cotta roof tiles, Junction City sewer pipes, and Crooksville bricks. The Roseville Pottery, founded in 1838, was the largest company by 1906. Twelve thousand gallons of stoneware jars per day came from the Roseville factory. They are also famous for "art pottery." Roseville and others produced many highly decorated pieces, including large umbrella stands, cuspidors, vases and flowerpots. The Ohio Ceramic Center between Roseville and Crooksville portrays the area's story.

Coal mining grew after the Civil War. Severe labor disputes erupted regularly. Shawnee became headquarters for the national labor movement of The Knights of Labor when it started recruiting members. Dissidents, however, preferred the new American Federation of Labor, formed in Columbus, and the Knights soon became extinct. New Straitsville is notorious for a disastrous mine incident in 1884. During a bitter conflict between strikers and strikebreakers, a gang loaded five mine cars with burning coal and pushed them down into the mine tunnels. A huge fire started in the mines that not only damaged the industry then but still burns through the coal seams.

Perry County honors naval hero Commodore Oliver Hazard Perry whose ships defeated the British in the Battle of Lake Erie in 1813.

PERRY
ST. JOSEPH'S DOMINICAN FRIARY, 1818

St. Joseph's was the first Catholic church in Ohio, and the first in the Northwest Territory. When I drove up over the crest of the hill and saw it in the distance, I knew right then that I'd paint it. This was the first painting I did for the Paint Ohio project. It was completed on site in the quiet of the graveyard.

–Debra Joyce Dawson

St. Joseph's Dominican Friary, 1818   18" x 24"   Oil on Canvas - Debra Joyce Dawson

Pickaway

2000 Population - 52,727
Land Area - 502 Sq. Mi.
Persons/Sq. Mi. - 105.1

The numerous mounds and earthworks left by the prehistoric Adena and Hopewell Indians are important all over Ohio. Various shapes and contents have given rise to much speculation as to their meanings, from ceremonial to defensive. The practical early white settlers to Pickaway County determined the large circle attached to a large square in mid-county would be an excellent enclosure for their new county seat. Accordingly, when the county formed in 1810, the town of Circleville was built within the "fortifications." The streets and alleys formed concentric circles around the courthouse. This planned new town was short-lived, however. Continued growth and the coming of the Ohio and Erie Canal demanded more room for the town and impinged upon the earthen ring. In 1838, with the state's approval, developers organized the Circleville Squaring Company to breach the walls and make the circle into a traditional platted town. The walls were gone by 1858. Another unusual mound near Tarlton is shaped like a Greek cross.

Prior to the permanent settlers, Pickaway had been a hunting ground for the Piqua tribe of the Shawnee nation. These Native Americans had two important towns: Chief Cornstalk's town, and the Grenadier Squaw Village ruled by his sister Non-Hel-E-Ma. During Lord Dunsmore's War, the Virginia Governor's troops defeated the Shawnees and quickly made a peace treaty with the local Indians in 1774. Treaty holdout, Mingo Chief John Logan, had been in favor of peaceful settlement until whites slaughtered his family. Logan gave an impassioned plea about his plight under the spreading branches of a huge elm tree on the Pickaway plains. Logan's speech is one of the most well known worldwide, and Logan's Elm, one of the largest elms in the U. S., was Ohio's most famous tree until it died in 1964 from damage by blight and storms.

Fertile because of its glacial till soil, Pickaway has been more than eighty percent farmland since its first settlers built cabins along an old Indian trail between Lancaster and Chillicothe. The canals, and later the railroads, ensured eastern markets for farm products. Slate Run Farm Metro Park is a living museum of typical Ohio farming as it was in the 1880's. At this agricultural park the workers and volunteers use period equipment to tend livestock and plant land that has been continuously cultivated since 1805.

The world knows Circleville for another tribute to agriculture, the Pumpkin Show. Celebrating its one hundredth anniversary with Ohio's Bicentennial, the harvest extravaganza has become the nation's sixth largest festival. Starting with one merchant's special produce display in 1903, today over 400,000 people enjoy hundreds of displays and activities, and eat pumpkin in every conceivable mix. Famous showman Ted Lewis, who wrote *Me and My Shadow*, was a child performer at his hometown's festival. During a six-decade career, he became the county's highest paid entertainer.

Pickaway is a corruption of "Piqua," a branch of the Shawnee Indian tribe. The word means a man who rose from the ashes.

PICKAWAY
MORNING WORK

Here's my tribute to the history of farming in Ohio, past and present. Slate Run Living Historical Farm is a working farm, frozen in the time of the 1880s. This painting was "given" to me; it flowed effortlessly from my brush on an extremely hot Saturday in July. While I was painting, Amy came out into the garden to pick tomatoes. I quickly sketched her into the painting before she moved away. Amy later came to look at the painting, and I asked her if she had any ideas for a title. She thought for a moment and said, "Morning Work. This is what I do in the morning before it gets too hot."

–Debra Joyce Dawson

Morning Work   16" x 20"   Oil on Canvas - Debra Joyce Dawson

Pike

2000 Population - 27,695
Land Area - 441 Sq. Mi.
Persons/Sq. Mi. - 62.7

A rural serenity permeates Pike County as it has for ages. Unlike most Ohio counties, Pike has had a minimum of violence and conflict in its past. Ample evidence suggests heavy usage of the prehistoric mound builders for ceremonial and community purposes, but not war. Archeologists document forty-four mounds, eight enclosures, nine burial sites, a cemetery, and two villages. One of the most curious is the earthwork near Piketon that is a circle and a square connected by twelve smaller circles and crescents. The Shawnee Woodland Forest Indians used the Scioto River through the county for transportation and hunting, but left the area peacefully by 1812. Pike County was chartered in 1815 with Piketon as its county seat.

Yoakum's Trace, which went from Portsmouth to Chillicothe and the longer Zane's Trace brought settlers mostly from Virginia, Maryland, and Kentucky. Hezekiah Merritt is purported to be Pike's first settler in 1795. The Eager Inn (1797), one of the first county buildings, opened at the intersection of Zane's Trace and the Buckeye Trail. The Inn later served as a stop on the Underground Railroad.

The first court sessions were held in Abraham Chenoweth's Piketon house. During the first term defendants were jailed in a sugar hogshead inverted and weighed down. Fortunately, air holes were punched in the sides. Piketon's brick courthouse opened in 1817; it still stands. Distinguished soldier and politician Robert Lucas married and moved to Piketon in 1820 where he opened a general store before returning to politics. Which brings us to the Pike County War.

Piketon was originally scheduled to have the Canal go through, but Lucas had property in Jasper. He happened to be Ohio governor from 1832-36, during the canal boom; not-too-surprisingly the route was moved to the Jasper side of the Scioto River away from Piketon. For the next thirty years the battle for the county seat raged between Piketon and Waverly, a town built expressly for the canal. The name comes from Sir Walter Scott's Waverly novels, favorites of canal engineer Francis Cleveland, President Grover Cleveland's uncle. Waverly entrepreneur James Emmitt aggressively campaigned for the county seat by offering incentives such as financing a road and a bridge and building a courthouse. He had prospered with the canal opening in Waverly, owning mills, distilleries, and the Emmitt House Inn and Store along with other properties. The battle raged with plenty of mudslinging and undercover politicking, but no bloodshed. In 1861, a county referendum brought an armistice. Waverly became and has remained the county seat. Emmitt made good on his promises, but the prosperity of the canal age was waning. The railroads, which had also bypassed Piketon, had arrived.

Agriculture and timber have continued to anchor Pike County's economy. The Piketon Uranium Diffusion Plant provided thousands of jobs in the latter Twentieth Century, but its future is uncertain.

Pike County is named for Brig. General Zebulon Montgomery Pike. He was a soldier and explorer who discovered Pike's Peak in Colorado in 1806.

PIKE
THE EMMITT HOUSE

This was a real challenge for me. I have been accused of never having "modern" elements in my work. When I told my friend Tom Harbrecht I was thinking of painting traffic lights, he said, "Do it!" So I decided to go for it with this one. The Emmitt House was built for industrialist James Emmitt in 1861. It is partly the work of Sally Hemming's son, Madison Hemmings, who claimed parentage by President Thomas Jefferson. It served as a tavern and store for travelers on the Ohio-Erie Canal that passed directly in front of it. Thank you to Doris Cooper for all of her help and input.

–Debra Joyce Dawson

The Emmitt House   20" x 24"   Oil on Canvas - Debra Joyce Dawson

Portage

2000 Population - 152,061
Land Area - 492 Sq. Mi.
Persons/Sq. Mi. - 308.8

From a transportation hub to an intellectual one, Portage County historically has been integral to Ohio's growth and development. Key Native American travel routes on and between the Cuyahoga, Chagrin, and Mahoning rivers lie in Portage County and the nearby Tuscarawas River. When the New England settlers arrived approximately in 1799, Portage was still centrally located amid trade routes from Cleveland to Pittsburgh and south to Columbus. The County grew as a dairy-farming region along with having small industries on the various waterways. The Pennsylvania and Ohio canal opening in 1840 cinched the movement of goods and services that accelerated county growth.

With good sources of silica, Portage birthed several glassmaking factories that prospered throughout the 19th Century. The Ravenna Glassworks was especially noted for its historical and pictorial bottles and flasks. The glass industry faded as cheap natural gas drew the companies to Pittsburgh and Toledo. Tanning and carriage works were also important industries.

The early 19th Century intellectual foments and reform came to Portage nearly as soon as it was settled. Ravenna founder Benjamin Tappan established the Historical and Philosophical Society of Ohio (now the Cincinnati Historical Society) in the 1830's. He was a U. S. Senator and president of the Ohio Canal Commission as well as an ardent abolitionist.

Franklin Mills (now Kent) was established in 1805. That year, John Brown moved there with his family. Always a dreamer, he tried several failed business ventures including trying to bring the silk industry to Ohio, a scheme which failed when the silkworms could not survive Ohio winters. By 1835, Brown left Franklin Mills to pursue other causes.

Schisms and reform among the Protestant sects in the early 1900's led to construction of many new churches and institutions to support them. The Disciples of Christ denomination was founded in Portage, and their school, the Western Reserve Eclectic Institute, opened in 1850. An early student, instructor and principal was future-President James A. Garfield. His words became the mission statement of the school: "...do you not feel a spirit stirring within you that longs to know—to do and to dare—to hold converse with the great world of thought and hold before you some high and noble object to which the vigor of your mind and strength of your arm may be given?" The Institute gained college stature in 1867 changing its name to Hiram College. Poet Vachel Lindsay helped with the college annual, "Spiderweb," when he and his sister attended Hiram. Noted for his uniquely American voice and strong rhythmic patterns, Lindsay wrote "The Congo" and "Abraham Lincoln Walks at Midnight" among many others.

Poet Hart Crane (1899-1932) was born in Portage County. Acclaimed as "Poet of the Jazz Age," Crane is most widely known for "The Bridge."

In 1910, Kent became one of Ohio's normal schools for training public school teachers. A comprehensive university since 1935, KSU now has seven branch campuses and numerous outstanding programs. The horror of the May 4, 1970, shooting of more than thirty students by the Ohio National Guard during anti-Vietnam War protest demonstrations led to establishing a Center for Peaceful Change. The Center and an on-campus park memorialize and educate all about the significance of the event.

Portage County is named for the old eight-mile Indian path between the Cuyahoga and Tuscarawas Rivers.

PORTAGE
THE HIRAM INN,
HIRAM COLLEGE, HIRAM

The Hiram Inn sits next to Hiram College in Hiram, Ohio. I liked its architecture because it has remained relatively true to its original design.

—Tom Harbrecht

The Hiram Inn, Hiram College, Hiram, Ohio 18" x 36"   Oil on Canvas - Tom Harbrecht

Preble

2000 Population - 42,337
Land Area - 425 Sq. Mi.
Persons/Sq. Mi. - 99.7

Hueston Woods State Park reveals much about the history of Preble County and Ohio. The shallow sea that covered ancient Ohio left trillions of sea creature remains in the dolomite limestone. Fossils are so numerous here that people from around the world come to collect them. The comparatively recent glaciers left fertile "till" when they last retreated. Prehistoric Indians left mounds such as the earthworks at Twin Creek.

More recent history has left its mark on Preble County, too. The remains of Fort St. Clair remind us of hard-won Ohio land. Built in 1792 as a supply post for General "Mad" Anthony Wayne's campaign against the Miami Indians, the fort lasted only a few months before Chief Little Turtle led 200 warriors in a victorious raid against Major John Adair's Kentucky militia. After a heated battle, six soldiers lay dead. They are buried under the "Whispering Oak." This massive tree still stands as a witness to the event. Folks say that sounds of the battle can be heard in the wind and rustling leaves of the oak as it whispers the names from the tombstones at its base: Williams, Jeff, Clinton, Bowling, English, and Hale. Chief Little Turtle left a positive legacy as a peacemaker after the Treaty of Greenville by urging the Miami to live peacefully with the newcomers.

A soldier who served with Wayne, Mathew Hueston, admired the land so much that he returned to the area in 1797 to settle. One of America's earliest preservationists, Hueston left a portion of the forest untouched, as did his descendants. Upon the death of the last of his descendants in the 1930's, Hamilton conservationist Morris Taylor held the forestland in trust until the State could buy it in 1941. These two hundred acres of Ohio's original forest remain today as a National Historic Landmark in Hueston Woods State Park.

The people of Preble County strive to keep their heritage alive. The Historical Society Reserve and Museum has brought several landmark buildings to its site near Eaton, the county seat. Seven covered bridges remain throughout the county. When the oldest and only remaining double-barreled covered bridge in the state, the Roberts Bridge (built 1829) burned, the entire county rallied to restore it and move the bridge to a safer location in Eaton. All can again share this legacy.

Favorite son writer Sherwood Anderson also left a legacy. Born in Camden, the Anderson family moved frequently and lived in several Ohio locations. Anderson's numerous short stories and novels reflect his boyhood in small Ohio towns. Most famous for his 1919 "*Winesburg, Ohio,*" Anderson left a large body of fiction and non-fiction. His legacy endures not only in his writing, but also in his influence on other American writers such as Hemingway and Faulkner.

Preble County also claims the Reverend Benjamin Hanby as a noted citizen. He taught at a singing school in New Paris. While living there he composed his "Up on the Housetop" Christmas piece, a favorite until this day.

Edward Preble's legacy for the county, of course, is his name. He was a heroic naval officer in the Revolutionary War and the war in Tripoli against the Barbery Pirates.

PREBLE
THE WHISPERING OAK,
FORT ST. CLAIR

The Whispering Oak is a majestic oak tree that is located adjacent to the site of Fort St. Clair. Six soldiers were buried beneath the tree in 1792 after a battle with Indian forces.

–Tom Harbrecht

The Whispering Oak, Fort St. Clair 30" x 26" Oil on Canvas - Tom Harbrecht

Putnam

2000 Population - 34,726
Land Area - 484 Sq. Mi.
Persons/Sq. Mi. - 71.8

Although French traders visited the Indian town Tawa as early as 1750, the swampy, dense forest area did not warrant American attention until the War of 1812. Prior to General William Henry Harrison marching troops northward to end the War on Lake Erie, the army built a rough stockade here as a supply post. Troops occupied Fort Jennings for several years, but saw no fighting. When the fort was abandoned, a town of Fort Jennings arose on the site, which may still be visited.

One of the counties created out of the Great Black Swamp region, Putnam was also part of the final home of indigenous Indians. Pushed into northwestern Ohio by the Treaty of Greenville, subsequent "agreements" and fighting pushed the Native Americans further west. Ottawa, the county seat of Putnam, is in the middle of the last land reserved for the Indians in Ohio. In spite of a treaty, the government put that five square miles up for sale in 1833; the new white settlement began in 1834.

At the core of Putnam County are two deeply held tenets, religion and land husbandry. Germans and Swiss built the county upon these enduring foundations. French missionaries had visited the area in the mid 18th Century and converted some of the Indians to Roman Catholicism. German Catholics were the first settlers to move in, led by a valiant priest. Father John Otto Bredeick brought a small band of pioneers to settle on forty acres he bought along the newly built Miami and Erie Canal. They organized a parish in 1848 that included Delphos and "Sixteen," later renamed Ottoville in his honor. The priest rode horseback between the two. The first church was erected in 1850 with the upper story as a church and the lower level for settlers to stay until they could build shelter. Ottoville became the main shipping point on the Canal, but also grew to be the center of the ensuing long-time "church wars."

The Catholics in Gandorf had the tallest church spire in the county. Realizing they could not compete with that height, the Ottoville congregation built a second spire. The double spires of Ottoville's Immaculate Conception Church are a landmark identifying the town from afar. Not to be outdone, the Kalida parish built St. Michaels with a separate bell tower in the Venetian style. Church life remains the mainstay of the rural life in this area.

More than ninety percent of Putnam County is farmland. The rich soil left from the drained swamp is ideal for most crops. The county is second in Ohio in wheat production and fourth in hogs. Growing and processing tomatoes is the largest enterprise in Putnam, which is the number one tomato producing county in the State.

Putnam County bears the name of General Israel Putnam, famed Revolutionary War hero. He is known for leading troops at the Battle of Breed's Hill (often misnamed Bunker Hill) in Boston in June, 1775.

PUTNAM
OTTOVILLE SUNSET

I went to Putnam County and toured six recommended sites, none of them churches. But the churches are what stood out for me in this flat county where you can see the spires from a long way off, like you can in Europe. The double spires of Ottoville's Immaculate Conception and the over 100-year-old Odenweller Feed Mill are silhouetted against a sunset, paying tribute to the beauty of nature, the power of man's faith and the fruit on one's labor. Thanks to Carol Wise and Millie Ruen for their history lessons.

–Debra Joyce Dawson

Ottoville Sunset 18" x 24"   Oil on Canvas - Debra Joyce Dawson

Richland

2000 Population - 128,852
Land Area - 497 Sq. Mi
Persons/Sq. Mi. - 259.3

Forces as old as the glaciers and as modern as Hollywood have shaped the Richland County of today. Glacial till enriched the soil while melting ice birthed rivers. The Hemlock Falls and Old Groveport River Bed Park provides a resulting ecosystem example. Two hundred million years ago the Groveport River flowed west from the Appalachians and turned south in what was to become Richland. Approximately 150,000 years ago the river was blocked by the Illinois glacier rerouting it to form today's Clear Fork River. As part of the foothills of the Appalachian Mountains, Richland benefits from the ancient geologic phenomena of upheaval that created that range, too. The Richland hills are the center of Ohio's ski industry with Clear Fork and Snow Trails resorts.

Prehistoric mound builders inhabited the area before the historic tribes such as the Wyandot who had a trading center at Mansfield, the county seat, until 1835. Although Richland became a county in 1808, it was still a dangerous wilderness. Early settlers included John Chapman, better known as Johnny Appleseed, who not only sowed orchards to anticipate pioneers' needs, but also acted as Indian liaison and information center. American forces erected a chain of blockhouses at this western frontier edge to protect against British and Indian attacks during the War of 1812.

Real growth did not reach Richland until the 1850's railroad boom. Industry also boomed throughout the Nineteenth Century. Buggies, steam tractors, pumps, stoves and other appliances were the basis for personal and county wealth. While various businesses have waxed and waned, Richland has been economically balanced between manufacturing and farming. One of the latest new ventures is the first wooden carousel built in the U. S. since the early 1900's, fashioned by Mansfield's Carrousel Works. It whirls sedately at the downtown Carrousel Park restoration district.

Hollywood involvement with the county is attributable to a monument and a man. Architect Levi Scofield designed the Ohio Reformatory in Mansfield to resemble medieval castles. The Gothic structure took ten years to build before it opened in 1896. The progressive (for its time) prison stressed rehabilitation over punishment. Closed in 1996, it is now a museum when not being used as a Hollywood set. The amazing complex has been featured in *The Shawshank Redemption, Brubaker, Airforce One*, and *Tango and Cash*.

Pulitzer Prize winning author Louis Bromfield first went to Hollywood to write screenplays and turn seven of his novels into movies. He then returned to his Richland County roots and brought Hollywood home with him. In 1939, Bromfield began reclaiming Malabar Farm as an experimental ecologically sound farm. Poor agricultural practices had depleted the soil and left the 1,000 acres exhausted. Bromfield pioneered the return to "natural" practices and was elected to the Ohio Natural Resources Hall of Fame. He built the 32-room Big House where he entertained constantly, bringing his Hollywood friends there. When the celebrities were there, Bromfield urged them to work on the farm. Stories tell of James Cagney selling vegetables at the farm's roadside stand and Kay Francis helping to birth a calf. Humphrey Bogart and Lauren Bacall's wedding at the Big House in 1945 is legendary.

Richland County was named for its rich, fertile soil.

RICHLAND
FARMHOUSE AT MALABAR

Malabar Farm spread out over large acres of lovely choices for paintings, and I ultimately settled into a hillside where a creek washed through and beside the Malabar Farm buildings until it met this white back house, which is the ultimate focus of my painting. The foliage, fencing and woodlands created a lovely resting spot.

–Kaye Michele Darling

Farmhouse at Malabar 18" x 24" Oil on Canvas - Kaye Michele Darling

Ross

2000 Population - 73,345
Land Area - 688 Sq. Mi
Persons/Sq. Mi. - 106.5

Farmer Mordecai Hopewell hardly could have imagined an entire civilization being named for him. The mounds in his fields were excavated in 1891; hence, the archeologists christened the mysterious moundbuilders with his name. Ross County has the greatest numbers of "Hopewell" earthworks in Ohio. The Hopewell Culture National Historic Park has some twenty-three mounds and a museum that attempts to unravel the culture that was at the same time sophisticated and illiterate. The mounds here all cover buildings; most of them are ceremonial burial sites. As happened throughout Ohio, farmers obliterated mounds as they cleared and plowed land. Camp Sherman further imperiled the Ross County collection before the park was built in the 1920's.

When Nathaniel Massie arrived in Ross County in 1796, his party was at least the third to settle and create a major town. The Hopewell lived here about 200 BC - 500 AD. Eastern Woodland Native Americans succeeded them. "Chillicothe" means "main town" in Shawnee; the newcomers thought it a fitting name for their new main town. Thomas Worthington arrived during the 1790's to survey land that his guardian received for military service in the Revolution. In 1807, he built his mansion, Adena, naming it with the Hebrew word meaning "places remarkable for the delightfulness of their situations." White House and U. S. Capitol architect Benjamin Latrobe designed the gracious estate. Adena is one of three remaining residences designed by Latrobe in the U. S. From here Worthington, his friend Massie, and his brother-in-law Edward Tiffin planned the State of Ohio and their roles in it.

Chillicothe was capital of the eastern part of the Northwest Territory and State capital of Ohio twice. The road to statehood was hard-won, but the first General Assembly met here March 1, 1803, for the statehood vote. The original Statehouse was used as the Ross county courthouse after Columbus became the State capital, but was razed in 1852 to make way for the current courthouse. The Chillicothe leaders went on to greater state service. Tiffin

was the first Governor, and Worthington was one of the two first U.S. Senators and also Ohio's sixth Governor. Later prominent Ross County politicians were 2nd Governor Thomas Kirker, 11th Governor Duncan McArthur, 31st Governor William Allen, and Lucy Webb Hayes, wife of President Rutherford B. Hayes. She was the first "First Lady," the first to use a telephone in the White House, and the first to hold the Easter Egg hunt on the White House lawn.

Chillicothe had a War of 1812 prisoner of war camp, named Camp Bull from a slang term for the English; the stockade held 300 prisoners from the Battle of Lake Erie. Camp Sherman was a World War I training camp outside Chillicothe that trained over 120,000 men. Half of them served during the war, but the Armistice allowed the other half to be discharged. The ground now houses a prison and Veteran's Hospital.

Ross County remained rural, but the canal and railroads brought industry to the area as well. Businesses included distilleries, pork-packing plants, and flourmills. Short horn cattle were important after county resident Felix Rennick first imported them to the U.S. Major paper production facilities are operated by MeadWestvaco.

Ross County was named by General Arthur St. Clair for his friend U. S. Senator James Ross of Pennsylvania.

ROSS
ADENA STATE PARK

It was a hot and incredibly bright day at the Adena State Metro Park. It was late August and the sun was high. I decided to set up in the shade, where it was cool and focus this painting on the difference of light and shadow. My artistic concern with this picture was to make cool colors (green) feel warm and hot colors (red) feel cool.

–Richard Otten

Adena State Park 20" x 40" Oil on Canvas - Richard Otten

Sandusky

2000 Population - 61,792
Land Area - 409 Sq. Mi
Persons/Sq. Mi. - 151.0

Sandusky County is worth fighting for. Prehistoric Native American trails crisscrossed the area, and then Huron, Mingo, Delaware, Seneca and other historic tribes traversed the area as well. The first road to go through the Black Swamp, now Route 20, grew from a muddy trail to a stone toll road by the 1840's. Bishop John Seybert, a famous circuit-riding preacher, brought Methodism to Ohio in 1785. He dedicated his life to riding these trails preaching 9,850 sermons and leading over 8,000 prayer meetings. Now the Ohio Turnpike brings people to and through the county.

Major George Croghan certainly did not want to abandon the spot either. He countermanded orders from General William Henry Harrison to surrender Fort Stevenson in 1813. With one cannon and 200 soldiers, Croghan repelled the Indian and British forces four times as big and won the day. The Fort is now Fremont, the Sandusky County seat. The cannon "Ol' Betsy" guards the courthouse. Sandusky became a county in 1820. The last of the Native Americans to leave were the Seneca who, in spite of an 1817 treaty, were moved from their reservation at Green Springs to Oklahoma in 1831.

Blessed with a combination of Black Swamp and lakeshore soils, Sandusky has thrived with vegetable and fruit farming. Perhaps this bounty inspired Charles Stilwell of Fremont to invent the square-bottomed brown grocery bag in 1883 that we use billions of each year. The attendant food processing plants are also big business. The biggest ketchup bottler in the world is the HJ Heinz plant in Fremont. Woodville sits on a bed of the purest dolomite limestone in the world. The stone is burned in kilns, then used for wall plaster. This substance is so desirable that President Truman sent a truck to get some for White House repairs when a railroad strike prevented its delivery. In the 1880's, the largest oil producer in the world was the western end of the county with over 8,000 wells.

Rutherford B. Hayes was enamored enough of his uncle's land that he moved to Spiegal Grove after he served his second term as Ohio Governor. Among other achievements Hayes was instrumental in changing his adopted town's name from Lower Sandusky to Fremont. He retired to the estate after his term as U. S. President. Hayes' family continued to live there after his death, but donated it to the state in 1909. Spiegal Grove is now the Hayes Museum complex including the nation's first Presidential Library.

Writer Sherwood Anderson, who grew up in Clyde, did not want to hold on to Sandusky County — he wanted out. He became infamous in his own hometown, Clyde, for his book *Winesburg, Ohio*. The novel was an unflattering picture of life in small town America that the townspeople in general disliked. Sandusky County now claims him for the literary genius he was.

Sandusky is a variant of Native American words meaning "cold water" or the Wyandot and Huron "Sa-un-dos-tee" which means "water within water pools."

SANDUSKY
PRESIDENT HAYES FREMONT HOME AND MUSEUM, FREMONT

I visited on a crisp clear autumn day. I liked the way the sunlight hit the varied shapes of the house. The front porch was also interesting.

–Tom Harbrecht

President Hayes Fremont Home and Museum 20" x 30"   Oil on Canvas - Tom Harbrecht

Scioto

2000 Population - 79,195
Land Area - 612 Sq. Mi
Persons/Sq. Mi. - 129.3

As river dwellers will assert, the Ohio River is both friend and foe to those whose lives are tied to it. From the prehistoric Native Americans to modern Scioto County residents, the Ohio and Scioto rivers have been vital. The Scioto River has been the entryway to the north for eons. The ancient Adena and Hopewell peoples left evidence in their mounds near Portsmouth of extensive trading as far south as Florida and north to the Upper Great Lakes. Mound Park features a horseshoe earthwork and Tremper has yielded a huge collection of ceremonial pipes. These animal effigies disclose to us the skill of the people and the sophisticated use of tools to create extraordinary animal likenesses: birds, turtles, bears, otters, and many other species important to them.

Several tribes of historic Indians also used the Scioto River. First, the Wyandot who had been banished from Ontario, then the Shawnee who emigrated from South Carolina and Pennsylvania, moved along the rivers to settle in Ohio. The Wyandots named the larger river Ohio, their word for "beautiful." The Shawnee gave us "Scioto," meaning "deer." The Shawnee built an important town, Lower Shawnee Town, on the west bank of the Scioto/Ohio confluence. The French also sought this area. General Celeron DeBlainville's expedition claimed all lands in the Ohio watershed for King Louis XV.

The first American settlement, Alexandria, disappeared after flooding. The survivors wisely moved up hill to establish Portsmouth, county seat of Scioto, which was chartered in 1803. The oldest house in town is the 1810 house where tanner Aaron and Mary Kinney raised twelve children. They planted one of the first vineyards in Ohio. Some of the French refugees who were cheated out of their land at Gallipolis were granted land by the U.S. Government in Green Township. They named their settlement Burrsvillle because Aaron Burr was their champion in getting this restitution.

Transportation on and energy from the water helped the county grow steadily. At first resources, especially minerals and timber, were the main exports. Scioto County's gray shale made the best paving bricks in the U.S. Sciotoville was established as a rail center in 1841 to ship bricks, clay, and mill products; Rushtown shipped out timber from both the Ohio and Erie Canal and the railroads. Although the forest was substantially depleted, the Shawnee State Forest, Ohio's largest, has made a strong comeback. Between the hills and the forests, the county is at the heart of the "Little Smokies."

The fifty-two Floodwall Murals in Portsmouth depict the County's colorful history. The 2,000 foot-long murals display not only events, but also famous people from the county. Roy Rogers, "King of the Cowboys," grew up as Leonard Slye on a farm in Lucasville. Branch Rickey started the baseball farm system and integrated the National League by signing Jackie Robinson to play for his Brooklyn Dodgers. Julia Marlowe was such a famed Shakespearean actor in the late 1800's that George Washington University awarded her the first honorary Ph.D. ever given to a woman. Jim Thorpe was the player/coach of the Portsmouth pro football team that became the Detroit Lions. Consummate politician Vernal G. Riffe, Jr. from New Boston served the most consecutive years in the Ohio House of Representatives, thirty-six, and the most years as Speaker, twenty, of any other Ohioan.

Scioto County takes its name from the Scioto River, which flows through and enters the Ohio River in it.

SCIOTO
SCIOTO VALLEY AT THE OHIO

Much driving and intertwining roads got us to the magnificent sight of the sun setting on Portsmouth, Ohio, resting on the valley of the confluence of the Scioto River and the Ohio River. The Scioto between the mountainscapes of higher ground was a wonderfully effective view, and a great idea for a painting. The Scioto has always piqued my imagination as a child, and I now was able to paint this grand spectacle.

–Kaye Michele Darling

Scioto Valley at the Ohio 16" x 36"   Oil on Canvas - Kaye Michele Darling

Seneca

2000 Population - 58,638
Land Area - 551 Sq. Mi
Persons/Sq. Mi. - 106.6

Many war veterans from various Indian wars and the Revolutionary War settled in Ohio. Seneca County's beginnings were unusual because prisoners of war were among the first settlers. The Treaty of Miami of the Lake in 1817 released people who had been captives of the Indians. Many had intermarried and did not want to return east, so they became Seneca County's first settlers. Seneca was on the forefront of the French and Indian wars and the War of 1812. The first permanent structure in the county was built at Camp Ball, a stockade and supply depot on the Sandusky River. Fort Seneca, now the town of Old Fort, also provided supplies to the War of 1812 troops. Louis Cass and Duncan McArthur negotiated treaties to remove the Native Americans. The county became official in 1820.

Soldier Erastus Bowe returned to Fort Ball to open an inn, the Pan Yan. He speculated that the newly built road connecting Lower and Upper Sandusky would attract travelers who needed to rest. Two villages grew up around the Fort on the west bank of the Sandusky, Oakley and Fort Ball. Entrepreneur Josiah Hedges, however, had a different vision so he built Tiffin in 1822 on the east side. Hedges practically gave land away to induce settlement so Tiffin would be the county seat. A bitter rivalry ensued; there would be no bridge crossing the river until 1833. Finally, Hedges bought Fort Ball and moved the post office to Tiffin. A bronze Indian Maiden statue marks the site of the Fort Ball spring. The villages united at last in 1850, no doubt aided by the railroad coming to Tiffin in 1841.

Fostoria, the other major town in Seneca, actually spans three counties. It was originally a trading post/general store run by the Foster family. As a sole-surviving son, Charles stayed home from fighting in the Civil War to keep the business running. He gave credit to every soldier's family during the war. When Foster ran for Governor, the Democrats tagged him "Calico Charlie" in derision. This strategy backfired when Foster supporters festooned everything around in calico — towns, band uniforms, and neckties. The popular

Foster won handily and became Ohio's 35th Governor. Later he was President Benjamin Harrison's Secretary of the Treasury.

Tiffin, in 1883, was the first city in the U.S. to have an electric plant. Thomas Edison gave an electric chandelier to St. Paul's Methodist Church; in 1884 it became the first building in the nation to be constructed with electric wiring. The chandelier still hangs in the church. An even greater economic boom — the discovery of huge natural gas deposits in Seneca — soon followed the amazing advent of widespread electricity.

Both Fostoria and Tiffin offered free or cheap fuel to industries, especially the glass factories. Several companies thrived during the blown glass era, but many closed or were relocated when the cheaper pressed glass became popular. Tiffin Glass, the largest area company, adjusted to many changes, producing from 1888-1980. The Summit Art Glass Company in Ravenna bought the Tiffin glass logo and still produces specialty ware under that name. Fostoria maintains the Glass Heritage Gallery, even though the company moved to West Virginia in 1896.

Agriculture, Seneca's mainstay, has evolved into agri-business with corn, wheat, and soybeans as main crops. Eighty percent of the county is farmland.

Seneca County takes its name from the Seneca Indians who had a reservation here from 1817-31.

SENECA
COLD RAIN

It was a cold November rain and the mist grew dense in the atmosphere. My subject, a snaking irrigation ditch, presented itself as a baroque dream. The light was soft and the rain bounced off the field suspended in mid-air. This scene quietly spoke to me, asking for me to capture its cool and subtle beauty.

–Richard Otten

Cold Rain 24" x 36"   Oil on Canvas - Richard Otten

Shelby

2000 Population - 47,910
Land Area - 409 Sq. Mi
Persons/Sq. Mi. - 117.1

The serenity of the farmland belies the struggle over hundreds of years to achieve that peace. Shelby County was very much in the middle of the brutal wars to establish Ohio's frontier lands for statehood. The Native Americans who lived here allied with the French to keep out the British and then with the British to keep the Americans away. French-Canadian Jesuit Priest Peter Loramie came to minister to the Indians and establish a trading post. By 1782, Loramie had befriended the Wyandots and Shawnees to the point that the Americans thought him dangerous. General George Rogers Clark burned the settlement. Loramie and the Indians managed to escape into Indiana. In 1793, General "Mad" Anthony Wayne rebuilt and used Fort Loramie for his campaigns, but it was destroyed in the War of 1812.

Hardin was the first choice for county seat when Shelby became a county in 1819, but Sidney grabbed it away with Charles Starrett's donated land in1820. The early settlers quickly cleared land for farming. Hundreds of Irish and German immigrants came to help build the canal and stayed. The Miami and Erie Canal's 1837 opening brought more settlers and markets for the farm produce. Loramie once more showed its importance — it is the summit of the canal and therefore the location of Lock 1 North and Lock 1 South. The lock remains at Lockington are remarkably intact showing the six sets of locks that it took to get to the summit. Lake Loramie was dug as a feeder to the canal; the lake area became a state park in 1949.

The east-west railroad through Sidney initially enhanced the canal trade, but the north-south tracks added in 1856 helped spell doom for the canal system. Trains are still important to the county although not as numerous. Originally the Bellefontaine-Indiana line ran right through downtown Sidney. The danger and inconvenience, plus the disastrous 1913 flood, led leaders to locate a rail bridge outside town. The Big Four Bridge is an engineering marvel, but it was erected at great cost. During construction the trestles collapsed at least twice killing three

workers, at least one worker fell to his death, and one fell into the cement and drowned. Pouring resumed almost immediately. Completed in 1923, the bridge serves as a monument to those who worked and died there.

Shelby citizens honor their Civil War veterans with the Monument Building. Today it serves as city offices. The Shelby County Courthouse also promotes civic pride. Built 1881-83, the ornate structure has four gabled facades, each with a statue of blind justice and her scales adorning the pediment top. It has been named a "Great American Public Place."

County residents have always been ingenious and hard working. One of the inventions that affects our lives today was Benjamin Slusser's road scraper in 1876. That and other road building equipment are still manufactured in the county. The "other" flight brothers, Edward and Milton Korn, built and flew their machine at their Shelby County farm in 1909. Still ninety percent agricultural Shelby leads Ohio counties in cattle, calves, and dairy. Honda, Airstream and Plastipak are three major Shelby manufacturers.

Shelby County is named for Isaac Shelby, a hero of the Revolutionary War and first Governor of Kentucky.

SHELBY
THE BIG 4

We arrived at Sidney, Ohio, with complete surprise at the many very interesting cultural, historical and aesthetic neighborhood settings all packed in one small town-city. The immensity of the Big Four Bridge and its counterpart history is remarkable. No sooner had we turned a neighborhood corner than we were facing a monumental bridge of huge unexpected arches and enormous pillars. It created the illusion of a diminutive neighborhood overwhelmed by this eccentric, giant bridge! Many stories are attached to the history of this amazing bridge.

–Kaye Michele Darling

The Big 4 24" x 36"   Oil on Canvas - Kaye Michele Darling

Stark

2000 Population - 378,098
Land Area - 576 Sq. Mi
Persons/Sq. Mi. - 656.3

Between the 1820's and the Civil War, the canal systems provided the means for moving products from Ohio's isolated frontier to markets. When railroads took over that function, the canals slowly died, as did many of the small towns that serviced them. Today, enterprising counties are using the canal remnants for education, recreation, and tourism. Stark and other northeastern Ohio counties created The National Heritage Corridor running between Lake Erie and Tuscarawas County. Stark's twenty plus miles of towpath and intermittent canal sections are at the heart of this project. Visitors can experience several aspects of the system including walking or biking the towpaths or riding in a restored canal boat at Canal Fulton near Massillon. Alongside a restored canal town, mules Shorty and Doc pull the Helena III for a trip into the past.

The region was a transportation hub long before Bezaleel Wells started developing Canton in 1806, the first permanent settlement in Stark County and its county seat ever since. Various Native American tribes battled for control of the Great Trail that connected Pittsburgh and Detroit and passed through the county. By 1795, however, the Indians had moved west. The county grew slowly until the canals created a boom, quickly followed in the 1850's by the railroads. Major industries sprang up in Canton as market access opened. The Hoover Company converted from harness-making to electric sweepers. Timken was making ninety-five percent of all automobile bearings by 1907.

Prosperity, of course, brought leisure time, even to the working masses. Stark County's real heritage is football. Teams created in the early 1900's to relieve the tedium of the factories competed with the college teams already playing. Competition soon led to paid teams vying for real stakes. In 1920, owners of teams from Akron, Canton, Cleveland, and Dayton started the first football conference that in 1922 became the National Football League. While Canton and Massillon lost their pro teams within a decade to larger cities, Canton's role as the birthplace of professional football was assured when the national Pro Football Hall of Fame

opened here in 1963. Stark County regularly has been a high school football powerhouse and produced several pro football greats, including Paul Brown. When he coached at Cleveland, Brown was the first to hire blacks into the sport. The game is such a way of life in Stark County that the boosters give every baby boy born in Massillon's hospital a tiny football.

Of the many noted people whom Stark County claims, President William McKinley and his wife Ida are the most celebrated. The twenty-fifth president, McKinley served as U.S. Congressman and Ohio Governor before he was elected to two terms. He was assassinated in 1901, early in his second term and is buried in a regal memorial in Canton. Ida inspired the National First Ladies Library, which is located in her childhood home where she and her husband lived from 1878-91 and which now honors forty-one presidential wives. Rosalynn Carter presided over its opening in 1998.

Stark County took its name from General John Stark. He was the oldest living Revolutionary War veteran in 1808 at the county's founding.

STARK
DOC AND SHORTY PULLING THE HELENA III

I had a ball painting this! It was the last weekend the boat would run for the year. I stood on the towpath, with two photographers and a reporter. They were waiting for me to get some paint on the canvas, I was laughing, answering questions and trying not to feel too much performance pressure, all this activity centered on the moment when those big horses rounded the bend and brought the boat toward us. I worked on location two days in a row and finished in the studio. The next day people passed by yelling they had seen me in the paper. The people in this small town are very friendly and they sure do love their boat. I took a ride, very quiet and smooth, no feeling like it. These boats and horses were the tractor-trailers of their day, and life for the canal men was not easy or romantic. Canal Fulton was the first place to restore a canal boat and put it back into the water. The canal is wider than it would have originally been, and the trees would have been cut back away from the canal. Many thanks to Rochelle Rossi and especially to Bret Stephan for his historical perspective.

—Debra Joyce Dawson

Doc and Shorty Pulling The Helena III 24" x 36"   Oil on Canvas - Debra Joyce Dawson

Summit

2000 Population - 542,899
Land Area - 413 Sq. Mi
Persons/Sq. Mi. - 1,315.4

As part of the Western Reserve Summit County was settled by New Englanders early in the 19th Century. This legacy of Yankee ingenuity would give birth to one of the world centers of innovation. Settlers lived peacefully with the Native Americans in the Silver Lake area from 1803 until the Indians joined with the British for the War of 1812. Sea captain Joseph Hart founded Middleburg in 1804, but it was swallowed up by Akron. Boston (1806) is the oldest village in the county. When the Ohio-Erie Canal work began Simon Perkins of Warren laid out Akron to be the town at the summit of the canal. After the canal opening in 1827, the area flourished with mills and transportation. Summit became a county in 1840 with Akron as its seat.

Matters of the mind were important enough for several local leaders to establish the Western Reserve College in Hudson, termed the "Yale of the West." Elias Loomis built the second observatory in the nation there in 1838. Cleveland scions persuaded the college to move its campus to Cleveland in 1882 where it eventually merged with Case University in 1967. Western Reserve Academy remains in Hudson.

From the start the county had strong abolitionist leanings. At the First Congregational Meeting House in Hudson (1820) member John Brown railed against slavery as early as 1837. The Akron house where the fiery abolitionist lived from 1844-46 is now a museum.

Summit County attracted immigrants from the eastern states eager to open businesses. Surgeon Benjamin Franklin Goodrich decided to manufacture his durable elastic rubber hoses here in 1870. He had perfected the process that made rubber flexible. Goodrich Zipper Boots, galoshes, led to coining the word "zipper" for their claspless fasteners. It was the first rubber industry west of the Alleghenies and was to spur Akron to be the "Rubber Capital of the World" well into the Twentieth Century. Seiberling started the Goodyear Company in 1898 after Charles Goodyear developed vulcanized rubber, and Firestone moved his company to Akron from Detroit in 1900. The Institute of Polymer Science at Akron University is leading the way for new materials as the rubber industry moves globally.

Although mostly associated with the automobile industry, Akron plays a big role in aerospace as well. Goodyear's blimps are famed. The Lockheed Martin Airdock built in 1927 is still one of the largest buildings in the world without internal supports. Lincoln Ellsworth was the first man to fly over both Poles in 1935. Goodrich made the original space suits. Firestone High School graduate Judy Resnick, the second woman in space, died when the Challenger spaceship exploded seventy-three seconds after liftoff in 1986.

The National Inventor's Hall of Fame honors and encourages innovations of all kinds. Barberton founder, Ohio Columbus Barber, established the Diamond Match Company that produced the first non-poisonous match in 1911, and also safety matches. Alcoholics Anonymous got its start in 1935, when Akron's William Wilson helped Dr. Robert Smith regain sobriety. This success led to others seeking help at Dr. Bob's house.

Summit County was named for being the highest point of land on the Canal, called the Portage Summit.

SUMMIT
ALONG EVERETT ROAD

I drove all day searching for Summit County's endless wonders. There were so many wonderful things to paint, I could not come to a decision. As I painted my last site — the Everett Road Covered Bridge — dusk began to set in. I began to pack up my paints and call it a day when I saw a storm roll in across the horizon. I stopped the car, set up fast as lightning, and frantically recorded the sight. Upon returning to the studio, the little study of the rain storm had so much mood that I knew it was my subject.

–Richard Otten

Along Everett Road 18" x 24"   Oil on Canvas - Richard Otten

Trumbull

2000 Population - 222,116
Land Area - 616 Sq. Mi
Persons/Sq. Mi. - 365.2

When General Arthur St. Clair declared Trumbull a county and Warren its seat in 1800, he started the first business, too. Warren became the Capital of the Western Reserve and as such, the site of its first land office and courthouse. Chosen because it had the most people of any settlement, five, Warren rapidly grew as settlers first trickled and, after 1812, streamed into the Reserve. Today's Courthouse replaced former buildings in 1897 and is the pride of the county.

Pioneer James Heaton also started a huge Trumbull County business with the opening of the first charcoal iron furnace in the Western Reserve at Niles. The iron and steel industries have defined the entire Mahoning Valley to this day. The growth of industry has been riddled with strife. As immigrants came to the area from abroad and from the South to fill the plentiful jobs, in the 1920's the Ku Klux Klan grew with its hatred of foreigners, African Americans, and various religious groups. Violence came after a KKK rally in Niles in 1924. The Klan was turned back and its heyday was over in the area. Violence occurred regularly as factory workers organized. During the Little Steel Strike in 1937, strikers were beaten and fifteen workers were killed during a protest in Niles. The "Little" steel companies did give in the following year, so the strike was not in vain.

The Packard family began an industrial dynasty in the late 1800's with an electric company in Warren. Their first automobile debuted in 1899. The success of the car allowed the electric company to thrive as well. Warren became the first city in the country to light streets with incandescent lamps. The Packard Company joined General Motors in 1932. As a leader in automobile electric systems, the company today is Delphi Packard Electric. Trumbull County's Warner brothers started a business dynasty of a different sort. Harry, Sam, Albert, and Jack opened their first motion picture theater in 1905 in Youngstown before moving to Hollywood and founding Warner Brothers Pictures in 1923.

True to its Western Reserve capital heritage, Trumbull has produced many politicians. Foremost was William McKinley (1843-1901) born in Niles. McKinley served in Congress and as Ohio Governor before being elected President. He was assassinated early in his second term. McKinley's reconstructed birthplace and a Memorial Library and Museum honor him in his hometown. Samuel Huntington and James D. Cox, Ohio's 3rd and 28th governors respectively, have roots in Trumbull. More recent U.S. Congress members James Traficant and Deborah Pryce both hale from Warren.

While not technically a politician, Clarence Darrow from Kinsman significantly affected the American political scene. Darrow is renowned for arguing separation of church and state in the Tennessee vs. Scopes trial. In Illinois vs. Nathan Leopold and Richard Loch, Darrow delivered what has been called the most eloquent attack on the death penalty ever in court. No client of his was ever executed. His boyhood home, Octagon House, is preserved for posterity.

Trumbull County is the named after the Connecticut Governor from 1797-1809, Jonathan Trumbull, Jr.

TRUMBULL
FIRST BUSINESS

The Trumbull County Courthouse is a magnificent structure. Quite beautiful in its place. The view from the bridge over the Mahoning River affords a classic scene; one I felt was worthy of painting. Lower, late afternoon light gave the stone finish a sort of golden glow. I was arrested by the view, a perfect painting. Hope I did it justice.

–Richard Canfield

First Business 18" x 24" Oil on Canvas - Richard Canfield

Tuscarawas

2000 Population - 90,914
Land Area - 568 Sq. Mi
Persons/Sq. Mi. - 160.2

Too often the best places to live have sad, tumultuous histories because of that very desirability. The Tuscarawas River Valley is one such place. The region was blessed with abundant forests and water and strategically situated between the Ohio River and Lake Erie. Native Americans traversed and fought over the area repeatedly. The Delaware tribe, displaced from its eastern homeland, occupied the valley with what is now Newcomerstown as their capital. In 1764, Colonel Henry Bouquet led British forces there and negotiated a brief peace with the Delaware, Shawnee, and Wyandot.

In the mid 1700's, Delaware chiefs gave missionaries permission to work with the natives. Most prominent was Moravian David Zeisberger who converted hundreds of Delaware. Schoenbrun was established in 1772 as a mission, followed shortly by nearby Gnadenhutten. Schoenbrun claims several Ohio "firsts": first settlement, first planned town, first civil code, first church, and first school.

The Revolutionary War and Indian skirmishes continued in the Northwest Territory. Fort Laurens, built in1778, was Ohio's only Revolutionary War fort. Winter weather, illness, and lack of supplies abetted an Indian siege; troops abandoned the fort a year later. Today there are no traces of the fort, but at the site, Ohio's Tomb of the Unknown Patriot of the American Revolution honors one of twenty-three fallen defenders.

Under enormous pressure to rebel from the British and other Native Americans, the converted Indians maintained neutrality. Finally, in 1781, the British and Indians rounded up all the Christians Indians. Conditions there were so bad in the captives' town that they begged to return to the valley to gather supplies. The one-hundred fifty allowed to go were ambushed at Gnadenhutten by Colonel David Williamson in 1782. All men, women and children were systematically murdered. The savage act was in retaliation for Indian raids in Pennsylvania, but these Indians were not involved. Only two boys escaped to tell the awful tale.

Settlers came steadily after the Treaty of Greenville, and Tuscarawas County was formed in 1808 with New Philadelphia as its seat. Religion continued to play an important part in county growth. Joseph Bimeler led a group of separatists to Zoar. Much like the better-known Shakers, their commune prospered admirably until 1898, when discontent split the community. Much of Zoar has been restored, joining Schoenbrun and Gnadenhutten as Ohio Historical Society sites. Sugar Creek has a large Amish population. Proud to be Ohio's Swiss cheese capital, the town melds Old Order Amish ways, such as blacksmithing and furniture making, with visitor attractions. Sugar Creek is also operational home to The Belden Brick Company, one of the nation's largest.

The Ohio and Erie Canal and the railroads kept Tuscarawas County growing. Manufacturing has been the mainstay for the last century. The Reeves family made its fortune in steel and galvanized sheet metal, becoming the County's largest employer by 1896. Their estate now is open to the public as a museum. County pride is also based on two famous citizens, Cy Young and Woody Hayes. Young moved here as a child and retired here after his amazing baseball career. Native son Hayes is revered for coaching The Ohio State Buckeyes to national prominence.

Tuscarawas County took its name from the river. The Indian word means "open mouth."

TUSCARAWAS
J.E. REEVES HOME

The J. E. Reeves historic Victorian home was an immediate attraction to me one late summer morning. The combination of the sun backed white clapboard walls, the large porch and windows, and the arrangement of exotic plants gracing the home was engaging. I was privileged to meet the gardener while painting this on site.

–Mark Gingerich

J.E. Reeves Home 20" x 16" Oil on Canvas - Mark Gingerich

Union

2000 Population - 40,909
Land Area - 437 Sq. Mi
Persons/Sq. Mi. - 93.7

What is a Buckeye? Where did that term originate? Is it some kind of nut? These and many others are questions outsiders ask Ohioans, with as many different answers. Union County has the answer. When William Henry Harrison ran for President in 1840, the delegation from Union County built an actual, small log cabin from buckeye tree logs for the parade to the state convention in Columbus. The cabin was festooned with buckeye nuts and raccoon skins. Otway Curry, Union County native son, rode the float on the cabin's roof, singing an original song that ended calling Ohio "the bonnie Buckeye State." While Harrison opponents ridiculed the display and the candidate, both the song and the nickname stuck and Harrison won the election with Ohio's help.

Much of Union County was a neutral Indian hunting region. The Darby Plains, which encompasses the lower southwest third of the county, were Indian cornfields. When white men began arriving, they hunted with the Indians peacefully in the forest northwest of the plains. Significant portions of the Darby Plains are in nature preserves today; the Big and Little Darby Creeks are listed as National Scenic Rivers. The area comprises one of the top five freshwater habitats in the United States, maintaining many endangered species of fish, mollusks, and plants.

Four covered bridges that have been in steady use since built in the late Nineteenth Century cover various streams and waterways in the county. Resident Reuben Partridge patented the original design of the four. While some alterations have been made, the spans have been well maintained. Partridge, ironically, died accidentally while building another bridge. His legacy rests in structures such as the 1873 bridge over Little Darby Creek on Old Ax Handle Road.

Spas for relaxation and health were the height of fashion across the nation in the 1880s and '90s. Magnetic Springs was a popular water-cure resort during that time. The spring water was said to give a knife blade enough magnetism to pick up a pound of nails. The town's popularity dwindled in the 20th Century with the advent of modern medicine. Today Magnetic Springs is a veritable ghost town of empty hotels and guesthouses, but the natural mineral water is still being bottled and sold.

Another export from Union County is its courthouse design. David Gibbs designed the Marysville courthouse in a hurry because the original plans for use of the land it is on called only for a new jail. That plan rapidly changed to a new courthouse to replace four buildings that had been used earlier. Finished in the 1880's, the courthouse spawned a political controversy, but has been periodically restored and serves Union County well. A twin of the building stands as the Henry County courthouse in Napoleon. Later, Gibbs sold the plans to other counties. One can see the same design in Marion, Washington Courthouse, and Hamilton.

Major development occurred during the last quarter of the Twentieth Century when Mr. Honda caused first a motorcycle plant and then two automobile manufacturing plants to be built northwest of Marysville. Virtually all of the Honda Accords and most of the Civics purchased in the United States since the mid-1980s came from those Union County plants, which are providing jobs to thousands of people in the area.

Parts of Delaware, Franklin, Madison, and Logan counties united in 1820 to form a new county; hence, the name Union County.

UNION
LITTLE DARBY CREEK
COVERED BRIDGE

This covered bridge is located just off Route161, west of Plain City. I decided to paint a view looking through the bridge (looking south). Around and through the bridge, you can see the flat rural landscape of Union County.

–Tom Harbrecht

Little Darby Creek Covered Bridge 20" x 20"   Oil on Canvas - Tom Harbrecht

Van Wert

2000 Population - 29,659
Land Area - 410 Sq. Mi
Persons/Sq. Mi. - 72.3

The pioneer spirit that drove immigrants to withstand incredible hardships in their quest for a home has endured in Van Wert County. Dredged from the Great Black Swamp after years of warfare with French, British, and Native Americans, the land in the triangle of the Maumee, Auglaize, and St. Mary's Rivers was open to settlement after the War of 1812. Van Wert became a county in 1820. Surveyor Captain James W. Riley, one of the more colorful pioneers, established the first county seat, Willshire, in 1822, naming it after the man who saved his life in Africa. Riley opened a gristmill and was elected to the Ohio legislature, but left the state to return to his seafaring life. Van Wert City replaced Willshire as county seat in 1838.

The Wabash-Erie and Miami-Erie Canals, several railroads, and the Lincoln Highway opened markets for Van Wert farm products. The county has been agricultural from the start with over ninety per cent of the land in farms. Soybeans are the main crop, but at one time Van Wert was the "Peony Capital of the World."

Cultural activities are a real source of county pride. John S. Brumback initiated the first county library system in the United States in 1901 with his gift of the Brumback Library building. His pledge included the stipulation that the people would provide the books and maintenance, thus formulating the first public tax support for libraries. The resulting castle-like building, complete with turrets, along with several branches in other towns, has been a community resource for over 100 years.

The Wassenburg Art Center, an "undiscovered jewel," is in the former home of the wealthy peony grower who donated it in 1954. Central Life Insurance displays one of the nation?s most extensive private collections of fire fighting memorabilia in its Fire Museum. The exhibit includes 600 antique fire toys, leather fire buckets and fire marks dating from the 1700's, and assorted fire engines.

The Welsh, who settled in Venedocia in 1848, left a strong music and poetry legacy. The annual Gymanfa Ganu (Festival of Song) draws people from across the country to sing and listen to hymns and folk music sung in the Welsh tongue. The concert is presented in their 150-year-old Salem Presbyterian Church.

Science has not been neglected in Van Wert. The yearly Farm Focus shows the latest in equipment and research, as does the County Fair. Delphos farmer and high school dropout Leslie C. Peltier, the "World's Greatest Non-Professional Astronomer," joined the Amateur Association of Variable Star Observers as a boy and sent monthly reports to the organization until he was eighty. He identified twelve comets, two novae, and 130,000 variable star observations in his career. Bowling Green University awarded him an honorable Ph.D. for his work in 1947. John W. Lambert from Ohio City produced the first successful automobile here in 1891. He also had the first car accident when he ran into a hitching post on his trial run. Lambert later held over 600 automobile-related patents.

Van Wert County took its name from Isaac Van Wart, one of the three captors of spy Major John Andre. The spelling change occurred because of illegible Congressional Records.

VAN WERT
THE BRUMBACK LIBRARY

Now here was a site I was dreading to paint. I had painted so much architecture that I was just tired of it. Yet once I started to paint, I really enjoyed doing it. The idea of softening the architecture by painting the tree branches was my intent. This site is the first county library in the United States and the model for all those that would follow. It has recently been restored, and is now in danger of being closed due to lack of funding. An 86-year-old volunteer gave me a lovely tour of the library after I finished painting. Very nice people in Van Wert County.

–Debra Joyce Dawson

The Brumback Library 16" x 20" Oil on Canvas - Debra Joyce Dawson

Vinton

2000 Population - 12,806
Land Area - 414 Sq. Mi
Persons/Sq. Mi. - 30.9

The very thing that makes Vinton County a favorite for visitors compromises economic growth for those who live there — rugged landscapes with beautiful scenery. With the fewest people of any county in Ohio, Vinton's animal population outnumbers the locals fourfold. Vinton does have the largest wild turkey population (about 6,000) in the state and over 10,000 deer. Other long-absent native animals, including bobcat and wolf are making a comeback. The second-growth forest makes Vinton the most heavily forested county in the state, appearing much as it did when settlers first arrived.

After the prehistoric Adena and Hopewells, modern Shawnee, Mingo and other Native American tribes passed through. They used the short leaf and pitch pines for pine tar and the glossy jet-black Zeliski flint for tools and weapons. English, Welsh, and Irish settlers began arriving in the late 1700's attracted by mineral resources. Iron ore, coal, and limestone were mined and refined for export. Vinton County was part of the famous Hanging Rock iron region. The trees provided fuel for six iron furnaces here, with the Hope Furnace being the largest. Buhr millstones quarried near Raccoon Creek were marketed worldwide and lowered United States dependence on foreign imports. The county seat, McArthur, began in 1802, but the county organized in 1850.

Timber and ores exhausted, the furnaces and mines closed by the early 20th Century. The remaining scarred land was too rugged for large-scale farming, but reforesting with white and red oaks, poplar, birch, maple and pine trees and man-made lakes have revived the landscape. Timber is now the number one industry.

Three man-made lakes enhance life in Vinton County. Lake Hope, the largest, is in Zeliski State Forest. Lodging, picnic areas, and hiking trails are among the amenities this state park offers. Lake Alma was originally dug by a coal baron for an amusement park complete with pavilions, boats, and rides. It was open from 1903-1910 before going out of business. The city of Wellston now leases the state park lake as their reservoir. Lake Rupert has remained a wildlife area famous for fishing. Zeliski and Tar Hollow State Forests comprise most of the county land as well as a large part of the Wayne National Forest. The longest creek in the nation at one hundred miles, Raccoon Creek also cuts through Vinton County. These abundant natural areas lure thousands of sportsmen, campers, hikers, and nature lovers year round.

Many county families have lived here for generations. More recent folks have moved here for the quiet beauty and clear water and skies. As one of the state's poorest counties, residents have made efforts to bring in small businesses and other development. The dilemma is that those who live there and those who visit do so precisely because of the serene rural lifestyle. The county slogan is "Nature at its best," and that is likely what its future will continue to be.

Vinton County is named for Samuel Finley Vinton, Ohio statesman and U.S. Congressman. He was known as the "Father of the Department of the Interior."

VINTON
LAKE HOPE

I painted the view from the lodge at Lake Hope State Park. It seemed to me at first sight a classic design with a panoramic view of the lake and distant hills. I enjoyed watching the vultures flying overhead and the small fishing boat in the distance on this warm autumn evening.

–Mark Gingerich

Lake Hope 30" x 18"   Oil on Canvas - Mark Gingerich

Warren

2000 Population - 158,383
Land Area - 400 Sq. Mi
Persons/Sq. Mi. - 396.3

The firsts or greatest does not make a county, so much as what remains. Warren County has a great deal of both. Located between the Miami Rivers, the area has been an ideal human location for centuries. Historians estimate that the prehistoric Hopewell Indians made over 10,000 earthworks/mounds throughout southern Ohio between 100 B.C. and 500 A.D., of which approximately 1,000 remain including much of what we now call Ft. Ancient. Evidence of sophisticated engineering skills and a huge trading economy exists here in its over 18,000 feet of walls. Building materials and artifacts found here include copper from the Great Lakes, minerals from the southern Appalachians, shells from the Gulf of Mexico, and obsidian from the Yellowstone Park area.

Warren County became official in 1803 with Lebanon as the county seat. The oldest inn and the oldest business in continuous operation in Ohio, the Golden Lamb, opened there that same year. The Inn boasts famous guests over its two hundred years including ten U.S. Presidents, and Daniel Webster, Henry Clay, Samuel L. Clemens, and Charles Dickens among others. Lebanon's 1805 log cabin post office is the oldest still standing in Ohio. The Western Star local newspaper is Ohio's oldest weekly and the oldest still publishing paper west of the Alleghenies. Downtown Lebanon has been well preserved along with nearby Waynesville; both are destinations for history and antique lovers.

Warren County is an important site of another group of settlers who left a substantial legacy, the Millennium Church of United Believers in the Second Coming of Christ, or Shakers. The small group who arrived in 1805 established their Union community west of Lebanon as the parent village for western Shakers. Their strange ways did not endear them to the Lebanon population and several unpleasant incidents occurred in the early years. One story is that after enduring many threats, the Shakers cursed Lebanon so that the town would not prosper. On the other hand, nearby Dayton citizens welcomed them, so the Shakers blessed Dayton. Could that be a factor in the subsequent growth of the two towns? The industrious religious sect eventually grew to own over 4,500 acres and 100 buildings here and fostered five other colonies in Ohio, Kentucky, and Indiana. They were an incalculable boon to Ohio agriculture introducing the Merino sheep, Shorthorn cattle, and their own breed, the Poland China pig. Over 4,000 Shakers lived in Union over its 107 years. One of the few remaining Union buildings is the Otterbein Home Center for the Aged.

Of the many county citizens' lasting contributions, two deserve special note. Jeremiah Morrow was Ohio's first U.S. Representative and the only one for ten years; he later became the ninth Governor. Dr. John Evans from Waynesville left a medical and educational legacy few can match. He was a founder and first president of Northwestern University in Evanston, Illinois, founder of the Chicago Medical Society, founder and president of the University of Denver. Further, Evans was the first governor of the Colorado Territory. Evanston and Mt. Evans, Colorado, were named for him.

Warren County was named for General Joseph Warren. He was a patriot killed in the 1775 Battle of Bunker Hill.

WARREN
THE MOUNDS AT FORT ANCIENT

This is a painting of Fort Ancient State Park. The park road cuts through a portion of the prehistoric mound complex. I liked the way the morning fog softened the autumn colors.

–Tom Harbrecht

The Mounds at Fort Ancient 18" x 24"   Oil on Canvas - Tom Harbrecht

Washington

2000 Population - 63,251
Land Area - 635 Sq. Mi
Persons/Sq. Mi. - 99.6

Ohio's first county honors America's first President and one of the state's principal benefactors. George Washington had a very real and personal stake in the settlement of Ohio, especially its first organized settlement, Marietta, for which he prepared the plans. Washington had surveyed the area and fought for it before authorizing the Northwest Ordinance. The actual New England immigrants, the "Forty-eight Immortals," were friends and soldiers who had returned from the War of Independence with few resources. They met in Boston in 1786 to form the Ohio Company and arrived by flatboat at the confluence of the Muskingam and Ohio Rivers in 1788. Led by Revolutionary War General Rufus Putnam, they commenced building Campus Martius to serve as protection and housing while the town was being

built. The Ohio Company land office was also there. Arthur St. Clair, new Governor of the Northwest Territory, arrived shortly thereafter to govern from the county seat, Marietta.

Among the esteemed pioneers was the Reverend Manasseh Cutler who was responsible for the anti-slavery provision of the Northwest Ordinance. His son Ephraim Cutler cast the single vote in the 1803 Ohio statehood vote that kept Ohio from making slavery legal. Washington County had a critical role in the Underground Railroad from 1790, when the road from Alexandria, Virginia, to Parkersburg, West Virginia was completed. Fugitive slaves crossed into Ohio through Marietta and Belpre before going farther north. Sixteen documented Underground Railroad stations are in the county.

While farming, especially vegetable and dairy, has played an important role in Washington County, industry and commerce have always been the economic backbone. From 1800-07, ocean-worthy ships were built in Marietta. The fully rigged ships sailed down the Ohio to the Mississippi to the open seas. The "Start Westward" Monument designed by Mount Rushmore sculptor, Gutson Borglum, memorializes Marietta as the "Gateway to the Northwest." During the steamboat's golden age, hundreds

of the sternwheelers arrived and departed from the levee. Today, the Delta Queen's voyages dock here and several others offer visits or rides including the W.P.Snyder, Jr., America's sole-surviving steam-powered stern wheel towboat. Visitors also can voyage up the Muskingam River through the historic locks. In 2001, The National Historic Engineering Society awarded this 1841 marvel as a great engineering feat along with the Hoover Dam and the Golden Gate Bridge.

Oil and gas were found in the Duck Creek Valley in 1902. The petroleum and plastics business remains a huge part of county commerce. The Silver Globe Manufacturing Company is the only place in America that makes those silver lawn ornaments. Belpre thrives as the "Baby Doll Capital" because of the Middleton Doll Company.

Washington has many firsts. Bathsheba Rouse, Belpre, was the first female schoolteacher in the Northwest Territory and Ohio in 1789. Catharine Ewing, "Aunt Kay Fay," operated the world's first public orphanage and worked tirelessly for Ohio to establish homes in every county. Among its four native-born Ohio governors, Marietta claims the first woman governor. Nancy Putnam Hollister was the 66th governor when she finished George Voinovich's term from December 31, 1998, as he

left for the U.S. Senate, to January 11, 1999, when Bob Taft was sworn in. C. William O'Neill is the only person who has served as Ohio House Speaker, Governor and Chief Justice of the Ohio Supreme Court.

Washington County was named for George Washington who was president of the Continental Congress when the county formed.

WASHINGTON
ALONG THE MUSKINGUM

While searching for just the right view of the historic riverboat town of Marietta, I chanced upon a footpath in a park along the banks of the Muskingum River that was pleasing to me.

–*Mark Gingerich*

Along the Muskingum 24" x 30"   Oil on Canvas - Mark Gingerich

Wayne

2000 Population - 111,564
Land Area - 555 Sq. Mi
Persons/Sq. Mi. - 200.9

Orrville's The J.W. Smucker Company has been a leading enterprise in Wayne County for over one hundred years. Their corporate image of hometown wholesomeness combined with solid American Midwest values seems nostalgic. Orrville's basketball legend Bobby Knight is a more modern American icon. If there is an archetype American place, it might be Wayne County.

Blessed with a varied terrain and great natural resources, the area was home to a series of earlier people long before white settlement. Adena and Hopewell prehistoric Indians thrived as evidenced by the numerous conical mounds and circular earthworks. Later Delaware and Wyandot tribes had many towns here as well, but gradually moved west as white settlers arrived. Wayne was the third county formed from the

Northwest Territory in 1796. The original county seat was a log cabin in Madison. Organized in 1808, Wooster became the new county seat.

Most pioneers came from Pennsylvania shortly after the War of 1812. Amish, Mennonites, Dunkards (German Baptist Brethren), and Moravians moved in. Finding great conditions for agriculture and religious tolerance, they then sent for family and friends from Germany and Switzerland. Naturally, they brought many of their customs with them. In December, 1847, August Imgarde cut down a spruce tree and decorated it, as was the Bavarian tradition. Legend says that this was the first decorated Christmas tree in America.

These farmers have tilled the land into a state leader. The first important crop was tobacco, but that gave way to grains by the mid 1800's. The Ohio Agricultural Research and Development Center continues as a research leader. Today Wayne County is first in Ohio in oats, hay, cattle, and dairy products.

Towns thrived as well. The oldest remaining residence in Wooster belonged to General Reasin Beall. Although not a native Ohioan, he fought with Generals Harrison and Wayne, serving as the latter's quartermaster. Liking the area, he moved here and served as Registrar of land offices for Wayne County and for

Canton. The house was once used as a college dorm, but is now undergoing restoration as part of the Wooster Historical Society complex.

The area flourished as the Ohio-Erie Canal and the later railroads provided the means to market products on a larger scale. Industries grew as well. Smucker has sold preserves and pickles from 1897. The Wooster Brush Company also dominated the economy after the mid-1800s. These growing industries attracted a black immigration after the Civil War. Their descendants form a substantial black community in this integrated region. A hundred years later local churches sponsored refugees from Southeast Asia who have also prospered. While not without occasional conflict, Wayne County has steadily embraced its diversity.

Culture, too, has a strong history here. Wooster College opened in 1870 as a liberal arts institution. From the beginning Wooster has championed the inclusion of women and various races. The famous musical program, The Ohio Light Opera, based there augments academic renown.

The Ohio Legislature chose Revolutionary War General Anthony Wayne to name the county after.

WAYNE
THE GENERAL BEALL HOME

The General Beall Home, located in Wooster on the grounds of the Wayne County Historical Society, has a stately presence. The cascading flowers and ornate porch also caught my eye.

–Tom Harbrecht

The General Beall Home 24" x 30" Oil on Canvas - Tom Harbrecht

Williams

2000 Population - 39,188
Land Area - 422 Sq. Mi
Persons/Sq. Mi. - 92.9

Williams County's newest village is Holiday City, incorporated 1998 in Jefferson Township. This upbeat name might apply to the entire county in several ways. Williams, however, did not begin with much festivity. As a part of the area disputed with Michigan, its state location was in flux until the Toledo War settlement. Bitter arguments over the county seat location ensued. Folks from the northern, secluded areas could not get to Defiance, originally part of the county, for legal work, so finally state auditor John A. Bryan offered money for the buildings if the state agreed to move the county seat to Bryan. Defiance residents pointed out the foolhardiness of building a courthouse in a swamp, but build it they did. Bryan's first courthouse needed replacing after thirty years, so once again political clout in Columbus kept the county seat in Bryan

with a special act to build a new courthouse. That modified French Baroque, Romanesque exuberance opened in 1891. The County, chartered in 1820, has since grown steadily with less conflict.

Prior to white settlement prehistoric Hopewell Native Americans built a mound group near Nettle Lake, the largest natural lake in Ohio. Later, Woodland tribes such as the Erie, Wyandot, and Delaware hunted and fished in the area before moving west. Highway 127 runs along the old Indian trail on the 10,000-year-old lake beachhead.

Some reminders of the early settlers in Williams County remain. The only known Quaker Meeting House in northwest Ohio and the Kunkle Log Cabin (1845), unique for its basement and birthing room, are open to the public in West Unity. The Hay Jay one-room schoolhouse (1901) in Edon allows kids to have fun with living history as they experience school life from earlier times.

Much of Williams' industrial base ties into transportation. Stryker's William J. Knight was one of the engineers on the 1862 Great Locomotive Chase. As one of only four Ohio cities to have an official airport in 1918, Bryan was a U.S. Post Office airmail stop between New York and Chicago until commercial airlines took over the routes

in 1927. The American high-speed train record, 183.85 mph, was set between Butler, Indiana, and Bryan in 1966.

The "fun" industry is what really draws our attention. Bryan is home to the Ohio Art Company, makers of Etch-a-Sketch. The Spangler Company has manufactured candy for nearly a century, the most popular of which are Dum Dum lollipops, Safety Pops, and Circus Peanuts. The town square in Bryan is famous for the family fun of Christmas lights and summer concerts. For over 150 years the Bryan City Band has played on the town square. The Band is the oldest continuously performing concert band in Ohio. The director today is nonagenarian John Hartman. A former music teacher, Hartman revels in the fact that he played in the Ohio State Fair Band in 1928 when John Phillips Sousa conducted it.

Williams County takes it name from David Williams, one of the three men who captured traitor Major Andre in 1780.

WILLIAMS
HAY JAY SCHOOLHOUSE

The outstanding element upon first seeing this historic landmark was the relationship of the simple structure drenched by the evening sun while catching the shadows of the nearby trees with the surrounding countryside. This scene gave me an image of light and life imagining the children of yesteryear jostling about the scene.

–Mark Gingerich

Hay Jay Schoolhouse 16" x 20"   Oil on Canvas - Mark Gingerich

Wood

2000 Population - 121,065
Land Area - 617 Sq. Mi
Persons/Sq. Mi. - 196.1

Millions of years ago all Ohio was under the water of the great ancient Lake Maumee. Traces of that period can be found all over the state in limestone-embedded fossils and various other land features. Known before development as The Great Black Swamp, the northwest section of today's Ohio is largely a remnant of that lake. This area was the last in Ohio to develop because of its topography and because various treaties, especially the Treaty of Greenville granted the area to the Indians. The treaties were short-lived, however, as white settlers forced out the Native Americans with other "agreements." Wood County was created in 1820 with Perrysburg as the county seat.

Hostilities on the frontier continued during the War of 1812. The British allied with several Indian tribes were intent on retaining trading and land

rights. Congress fortified the Maumee Valley with a string of forts to repel these attacks including Fort Meigs at the foot of the rapids in Perrysburg in 1813. The swampy terrain made refortifying and resupplying the troops extremely difficult. The main trail for troops and supplies from Perrysburg to Fremont, approximately following U.S. Route 20, was called Mud Pike. Congress gave the unimproved road to Ohio in 1838. The road was known as one of the worst roads in North America. In spite of its logistical difficulties troops at Fort Meigs repelled two attacks before the enemy moved on towards Lake Erie. Today the Fort is one of the largest reconstructed walled forts in America.

With the draining of the swamps exposing rich soil, Wood County became an agricultural leader by the late 1800's. The land from the bottom of the sea yielded more resources for the county — oil and natural gas deposits. One boomtown, Cygnet, produced 208 million gallons from 1886-1900 piped to Chicago and New York, as much at the time as the rest of Ohio. Bowling Green, the county seat since the 1870's, also grew rapidly with 14,000 wells and 1,000 derricks by 1896. Bowling Green was nicknamed "Crystal City" because five glass-making companies started up there when offered free gas. The oil and gas boom was over by World War I.

Wood County has continued its agricultural heritage. Over three-fourths of county land is farms. Soybeans and corn remain important crops, and Wood leads the state in wheat. Food processing is also a major economic factor, especially tomato processing. Bowling Green entrepreneur Emerson Cain gave a new wrinkle to potatoes when he invented the first rippled potato chip in the 1940's. He named the new product "marcelle chips" after the popular wavy hairstyle of the period.

Wood County owes much of its modern recognition to Bowling Green State University. Established as a state normal school in 1910 to serve the northwest region of the state in training teachers, BGSU added other programs rapidly and achieved university status in 1935.

Wood County got its name from U.S. Army Engineer Eleazer D. Wood. While serving on the staff of Gen. William Henry Harrison, Wood built Fort Meigs.

WOOD
FORT MEIGS

Fort Meigs sits on a bluff overlooking the Maumee River in Perrysburg, Ohio. I wanted to include part of its structure, a blockhouse and part of the wall, to get a sense of its position relative to the Maumee.

–Tom Harbrecht

Fort Meigs 18" x 30"   Oil on Canvas - Tom Harbrecht

Wyandot

2000 Population - 22,908
Land Area - 406 Sq. Mi
Persons/Sq. Mi. - 56.5

The last group of Native Americans living on their homeland left Wyandot County in 1843. After Indians inhabited the area for hundreds of years, the U.S. government closed The Grand Reserve and relocated the seven hundred Wyandots to Kansas. The County officially formed in 1845 with the reservation area, now Upper Sandusky, the county seat.

Besides their name the Wyandots left their mission and a mill. The first Methodist mission in North America was established on the reservation by the Reverend James Findley. He also oversaw building a school, store, and farm. In 1816, a free Black itinerant preacher, John Stewart, came to Ohio territory to bring Christianity to the Native Americans. Eventually he reached the Wyandots and served at the Methodist Mission here from 1821-27.

During his tenure, the tribe built a new limestone Mission Church in 1824. A visitor today can still attend periodic services in this building and see the nearby burial ground. The mill is now the first museum dedicated to milling in the United States.

As in much of Ohio, prehistoric Indian evidence also exists in the county. The recently discovered (1990) Sheridan Cave in the Indian Trail Caverns near Carey has a large paleontological, geological, and archeological find from the last glacial period. Included are the remains of over seventy extinct non-native animals. Flint tools suggest human activity as well.

The Harrison Trail followed an ancient path from central Ohio to Lake Erie long before General Harrison used it for troops and supplies. The McCutcheon Overland Inn served travelers from 1829. The original log cabin behind the 1840's addition is being rebuilt; the chimney is mostly original. Charles Dickens, famous English author and speaker, wrote about the county's only inn in his *American Notes* after a visit in 1842. Almost a century later, the Lincoln Highway, America's first transcontinental highway, went through Wyandot County in 1913.

Most visitors today come to experience the Shrine of Our Lady of Consolation in Carey. The first settlers to the area were mostly German and Protestant. The few Catholics, however, eventually needed a church, which opened in 1875. The parishioners ordered a statue of the Virgin Mary and Infant Jesus from Europe. When it arrived during a raging thunderstorm, the procession made the entire seven-mile walk untouched by the rain. Hundreds of witnesses gathered in the town for the amazing sight. The site has been a shrine ever since and grown to be a major pilgrimage destination for thousands of people from all over the world searching for cures and/or salvation. Run now by Franciscans who arrived in 1916, the Shrine visitation peaks in August with the Feast of the Assumption in the huge basilica that replaced the original small church. While the influx of out-of-towners can stretch the small town of Carey and surrounding mostly rural county, the residents appreciate the ways lives are changed by their parish.

Wyandot County is named for the Wyandot Indians. They were the last tribe to cede their lands to Ohio.

WYANDOT
**MCCUTCHEN OVERLAND INN
(CIRCA 1829)**

I was thrilled to receive six recommendations from this county. I viewed them all. The Overland Stage Inn was not one of them. I had just decided to paint the Indian Mill when I received an e-mail asking me to look at the Overland Inn. Originally there was a log cabin (recently torn down but being rebuilt), and the Inn was added on about 20 years later. I liked the look of the original freestanding chimney and picked this angle because I had a good view of it. It was 24 degrees and sunny the morning that I painted at this site. My fingers and toes were numb at the end of three hours.

–Debra Joyce Dawson

McCutchen Overland Inn (circa 1829) 18" x 24" Oil on Canvas - Debra Joyce Dawson

SPONSORSHIP:

The success of this project can be directly linked to the support of the many individuals, institutions, and organizations that generously contributed their time, resources, wisdom and enthusiasm to make the exhibit, auction, books and prints possible. We also want to thank each county and people in them who believed in this project enough to offer support to the artists, by contributing $250 to the artist in their county. These were, in the projects early stages, the lifeblood for us in many instances.

IN KIND DONATIONS

Dr. Louis A. Zona, Executive Director – The Butler Institute of American Art, Youngstown
David Aronowitz, – General Counsel, O. M. Scott Corporation, Columbus
David L. Keister, – Attorney at Law, Columbus
Sharon Weiss – Sharon Weiss Gallery, Columbus
Bryan Roberts – The Bryan H. Roberts Gallery, Columbus
Bill Harkins – Hammond Harkins Galleries, Bexley
Barb Unverferth, Gail Burkart – Art Access, Bexley
Craig Hackman – Hackman Frames, Columbus
OZONE STUDIOS – Columbus
Michael Delgrosso – OZONE Studios, Columbus
Adam Bonner – OZONE Studios, Columbus
Don Olshavsky, President – ColorPlus, Lab Services, Columbus
Carol Potter, Marketing Director, Mill Creek MetroParks, Youngstown
Baesman Printing – Ray Laubacher, Corey Frix, et al, Hilliard
C. Gilbert James, Jr., Canfield
Robert Keeley, Columbus
Brad Dresbach, Stimuli Marketing, Columbus
Sam and David Schnaidt, Apple Tree Auction Center, Newark
Lute Harmon, Karen Matusoff, Ohio Magazine, Cleveland
The Cleveland Clinic Foundation, Rosalind Strickland, Teresa Dechant, et al, Cleveland
Becky Wildman, Manager, Statehouse Museum Shop, Columbus
Cindy Cline, Capitol Club, Columbus
Cincinnati Museum Center, Charlie Howard, Melanie Buxton, Cincinnati
Salem Community Center, Eric Greene, Mindy Strawn, et al, Salem

ARTIST'S SPONSORSHIPS

BROWN	- Jerry and Hylda Strange, Ripley
CARROLL	- Carl Saltsman and the Carroll County Historical Society
COLUMBIANA	- The Salem Preservation Society, Salem
	- Bruce Greenamyer, Bruce's Place, Salem
	- Salem H. S. National Art Honor Society, Chapter 625, Salem
COSHOCTON	- Brent Osborne, Columbus
ERIE	- Erie County Historical Society, Janet Senne
FAIRFIELD	- Lancaster Arts Festival, The Decorative Arts Center, Lancaster
FRANKLIN	- Craig Hackman, Hackman Frames, Columbus
FULTON	- Fulton County Historical Society
	- Edward and Carol Nofziger, Wauseon
HANCOCK	- Rieck's Framing, Findlay
JACKSON	- Jackson County Historical Society
LOGAN	- Logan County Historical Society
LAWRENCE	- Lawrence Country Historical Society, Robert Price, Naomi Deer
MAHONING	- Richard and Elaine Winkle, North Lima
	- Geo. P. Reintjes Company, Youngstown
	- Joseph and Becky Greasel, Salem
	- Jeffery and Paula Shank, North Lima
MARION	- Carl F. Hughes, President, The Fahey Bank, Marion
	- James L. and Joanne Traveline, Marion
MERCER	- Joyce Alig, Mercer County Historical Society, Celina
PAULDING	- John Paulding Historical Society Inc., Anita Bert
SUMMIT	- Summit County Historical Society
TUSCARAWAS	- Fred Miller, Tuscarawas County Historical Society
VINTON	- Lawrence McWhorter, Vinton County Historical Society, Hamden
WYANDOT	- Christie Raber et al, for the Wyandot County Historical Society

CONTRIBUTORS:

The research required for this project was monumental. To contact each county organization and people and places in them could not have been accomplished by our meager staff without the willing attitudes and kind support of the contributors in their respective counties. Though this is I know for certain an incomplete list even the unnamed have our sincere heartfelt thanks and gratitude. I know you know who you are, thank you. The following is an attempt to remember and thank those who were involved in a myriad of ways

I will have to start with Todd A Berry, a good friend and selfless helper, above and beyond applies. Many thanks to Governor Bob Taft and our gracious First Lady Hope Taft for the obvious and much behind the scenes assistance and encouragement. The friends and family of all the artists, for their sacrifices and encouragement. Judy Hoberg, what could possibly be said, that might be adequate? We love you. Martin Dawson, thanks and continuing thanks. Bob Otten thank you sir for your help and interest. Bob and Mary Harman, Stan and Kaye Darling, God bless you folks. Brent Osborne and Dave Hammond, you got us started with OHS, thanks. The wonderful ladies of Salem, Janis Yereb and Hope Theiss must be remembered. There were a number of people from all of the various sites, from volunteers to management that dug in and made things happen, most of whose names I don't know because we only saw them passing in the halls offering enthusiastic smiles. Then of course there are all the people in the 88 counties who offered so much; Belmont Co. - Terry Larrimer; Brown Co. - Judith Gray, Susannah West and The Dengler's; Darke Co. - Sue Detling Terry & Julie Clark; Guernsey Co. - Kurt Tostenson, Curator, Guernsey County Museum; Hamilton Co. - Ruby Rogers, Director Cincinnati Historical Society Library; Holmes Co. - Harley and Mary Neuenswander; Jefferson Co. - Charles Green and Eleanor Naylor, William Croskey, site manager of The First Federal Land Office, Steubenville, LaDonna & Richard Delatore; Licking Co. - Jim Kingery, site manager, Newark Earthworks; Lorain Co. - Bill Bird, Executive Director of The Lorain County Historical Society; Monroe Co. - Robert Indermuhle, Monroe County Historic Society; Perry Co. - Thanks for being the first county to respond for Debra Joyce Dawson; Pickaway Co. - Amy Flory, Slate Run Living Historical Farm' Pike Co. - Doris Cooper, Secretary, Pike County Historical Society; Putnam Co. - Carol Weiss, Director of Putnam County Historical Society, Millie Ruen; Stark Co. - Bret Stephan, Canal Fulton Heritage Society; Wyandot Co. - Christie Raber, then Director of Wyandot County Historical Society, now with the Wood Co. Historic Society; Van Wert Co. - Jeanne Zeigler; Fulton Co. - Debbie Sauder David, Director Sauder Village, and of course Carol Nofziger and Ed who made major contributions to my sanity and keeping me focused, thanks again and again; Franklin Co. Gary Wannamacher and Matt Smith for organizational assistance, and also to my own personal computer "Yoda" Corey Frix, thanks.

If one were to measure the cost of all the help given the time devoted to tasks at hand, the great ideas and immense cache of knowledge spent to accomplish everything to date, it would boggle the mind. Nevertheless, it must be said that though most of this help was offered in passing, with a "why don't you" or "did you ever think about" or "hey what if," "did you try" . . . in those passing moments, great thoughts mushroomed into what we now have come to know as "The Land We Call Ohio." And you all are a major part of it.

AUTHOR'S NOTES *&* ACKNOWLEDGEMENTS

DEBORAH BRADFORD LINVILLE

What a journey this project was! Through time and territory, tribes and treaties, trails and tributaries, I have traveled Ohio. As many other travelers have noted, Ohio is a state for meandering. Every long stretch of apparent sameness of landscape has turns and alternative routes with major and trivial stops abounding. Each historical and actual byway has its distinctive features at the same time that it connects to the whole. A traveler cannot hope to take in the entire perspective; she can only pick and choose that which appeals to her from the sites and stories of the trip. Heartfelt thanks to all my companions on the journey, the wonderful artists and project managers of The Land We Call Ohio for their information and inspiration.

A very special acknowledgement must go to the people of the Ohio Historical Society, who not only provided multiple reference resources for the project, but also encouragement. The State of Ohio has been an incredible source as well. The project was made possible by the hundreds of webmaster and website contributors who continually add to Ohio lore and share it so willingly. I urge all those interested in all things Ohio to visit the city and county historical societies, libraries, Chambers of Commerce, Visitor and Convention Bureaus, and genealogical websites for their wealth of information and links to more. All of us owe a tip of the beaver hat to 19th Century historian Henry Howe whose research and recollections inform anyone interested in Ohio.

Raised in Virginia, Deborah Bradford Linville became a Buckeye when she graduated from Ohio Wesleyan University, later adding a degree from The Ohio State University. She has been a teacher, administrator, publicist, and writer. Ms. Linville lives in Columbus.

JOHN W. HOBERG

John W. Hoberg is pursuing his new passion of being a videographer, having retired in 1999 after 30 years of practicing law with Vorys, Sater, Seymour and Pease in Columbus as an environmental attorney representing the regulated community. John was born in Lakewood, spent his early years in Chicago and his teenage years in southern England before attending Ohio Wesleyan University where he majored in U.S. History. He went to law school at the University of Michigan before joining Vorys, but now roots for the Buckeyes and loves Ohio. Judy, his wife of 36 1/2 years, is an artist and manager of Studios on High in the Short North arts district where Richard Canfield works with her. It was through this association John was introduced Canfield, and together they became excited about The Land We Call Ohio project. John is Chief Administrator and Executive Producer of the project.

MEET THE ARTISTS

RICHARD M. CANFIELD

Richard, originally from Youngstown, has lived in Columbus for 14 years. He is a co-op member of Studio's On High in Columbus and represented by Sharon Weiss Gallery on Lincoln Street in the Short North Arts District. He received his education and degree from The Art Institute of Pittsburgh, during which time he participated in a European summer study program with earth sculptor Angelo Cioti. He received personal instruction from friend and internationally acclaimed painter Henry Koerner, who along with Ben Shawn developed the "fantasy realism" genera. After graduation he served for two years as an instructor in drawing and painting at the Art Institute. From graphic design studio owner/operator to freelance designer, and salesman for the printing industry, Richard has enjoyed a twenty-five year career in various aspects of the advertising and graphics industry. In addition to his involvement as project manager with this project he is currently pursuing his interests and career as a painter.

KAYE MICHELE DARLING

Michele, a Columbus native, received her B.F.A. and M.A. in Art Education from The Ohio State University. She attended the Academie de la Grande Chaumiere in Paris, the Maryland Institute in Baltimore, and rounded off her education at the Columbus College of Art and Design (CCAD). Michele currently teaches art at CCAD and Fort Hayes Metropolitan Education Center. Her own art expression takes the form of paintings and drawings in a broad range of media. Michele's recent oils as seen in "The Land We Call Ohio" project are quite unique and her style speaks with a strong singular voice. Kaye Michele's work has been acquired by private collectors throughout the country.

DEBRA JOYCE DAWSON

A Native of Maryland, Debra has been living in Pataskala, Ohio since December 1989. Painting in oils for the past 41 years, Debra is also a printmaker. She received her formal training in Maryland and New Jersey by supporting herself and her two children as a typesetter and a full time professional singer. Marriage brought Debra to Ohio where she returned to the study of art at Denison University in Granville, and at The Columbus College of Art and Design. Since that time, art has been her focus.

Experiencing different cultures is an important part of Dawson's personal and artistic life. She has traveled and painted extensively in Europe, Asia, Puerto Rico, and in 45 of America's 50 states, and her works are in collections around the U. S., England and New Zealand. As a founding member of the Ohio Plein Air Society, Dawson has been back on the road, this time in Ohio, completing this present project. In addition to the Paint Ohio Project, Debra has just returned from a month long plein air painting excursion to England and to the Burgundy Region of France. An exhibition of work from this trip is planned for 2004 at the Sharon Weiss Gallery, in Columbus, Ohio.

MARK GINGERICH

Mark was born in West Germany and has studied at the North Light Art School, the Atelier du Nord School of Classical Realism, and Columbus College of Art and Design. In large measure, however, he is a self-taught artist. During the course of his career, he has turned increasingly to the plein air impressionist tradition. Working on site, he often develops smaller paintings or color studies that may give way to major pieces on the same subject or theme in studio. This is a method of working adopted by many of the great 19th century painters. Gingerich's inspiration comes, most notably, from the works of Barbizon painters Jean Baptiste Corot and Charles Daubigny.

Mark recently has studied with several prominent plein-air painters in the Midwest. He has had a number of solo and group exhibitions and is represented in Columbus by Bryan H. Roberts Gallery, in Bexley Ohio. Although he paints on a nearly full-time basis, Mark, blessed as a husband and father of five, supplements his full time painting career with work as a skilled brick mason.

Tom Harbrecht

Tom is an Ohio native who graduated from Worthington High School, Otterbein College with a B.A. in Physical Education and Math, and Marshall University in West Virginia with an M.S. in Physical Education. He has been a high school teacher and coach, Naval Officer in the U.S. Navy SEAL Teams, a technical advisor for Orion Pictures, and most recently a freelance artist and illustrator. The variety of Tom's past careers adds an interesting dimension to his work. Tom's inspiration comes from the many places he has lived. His paintings range from landscapes, seascapes to cityscapes.

After returning to Ohio, Tom headed back to school to pursue a career as an artist. He obtained a B.F.A. in painting and drawing from Columbus College of Art and Design and has been making art ever since. Tom's art depicts his fascination with the sea and American landscape, many from central and southeastern Ohio. His work invokes nostalgia of old houses, favorite vacation spots, or a peaceful country drive.

RICHARD OTTEN

Richard was born in Cleveland, and as a child learned painting from his mother, a studying artist. Relocating early on, Richard graduated from Worthington Kilbourne High School and received an Honors Diploma in Fine Art from Fort Hayes Metropolitan Education Center. He graduated with a B.F.A. Honors from Columbus College of Art and Design, and teaches painting in the high school program at CCAD. Chosen "Artist in Residence" for the Lancaster Arts Festival, 2002, Richard went on that year, as a Full Fellowship Scholar, to study at the Chautauqua Institute with esteemed faculty and students from around the world. Richard has participated in group shows across the country. His work focuses on Ohio landscapes. He is presently represented by Art Access of Bexley, Ohio.

SOURCES

Columbus Dispatch, ed. Our Counties, Our Homes. Columbus: Dispatch Printing Company, 2003.
Knepper, George W., The Official Ohio Lands Book. Columbus: Auditor of the State of Ohio, 2002.
Ohio Historical Society, ed. Marking Ohio's History. Columbus: Ohio Historical Society, 2002.
Traylor, Jeff., Ohio Pride. New Washington, Ohio: Backroad Chronicles, 1990.
Vonada Damaine, Amazing Ohio. Wilmington, Ohio: Orange Frazier Press, 1989.
Ohio Matters of Fact. Wilmington, Ohio: Orange Frazier Press, 1990.